Giving it up

Text copyright © Maggi Dawn 2009
The author asserts the moral right
to be identified as the author of this work

Published by
The Bible Reading Fellowship
15 The Chambers, Vineyard
Abingdon OX14 3FE
United Kingdom
Tel: +44 (0)1865 319700
Email: enquiries@brf.org.uk
Website: www.brf.org.uk

ISBN 978 1 84101 680 1

First published 2009
10 9 8 7 6 5 4 3 2 1 0
All rights reserved

Acknowledgments
Unless otherwise stated, scripture quotations are taken from the New Revised Standard Version
of the Bible, Anglicised Edition, copyright © 1989, 1995 by the Division of Christian Education
of the National Council of the Churches of Christ in the United States of America, and are used
by permission.

Scripture quotations taken from the Revised Standard Version of the Bible, copyright © 1946,
1952, 1971 by the Division of Christian Education of the National Council of the Churches of
Christ in the United States of America, are used by permission.

Scripture quotations taken from the Holy Bible, New International Version, copyright © 1973,
1978, 1984, 1995 by International Bible Society. Used by permission of Hodder & Stoughton
Publishers, a division of Hodder Headline Ltd. All rights reserved. 'NIV' is a registered trademark
of International Bible Society. UK trademark number 1448790.

Extracts from the Authorised Version of the Bible (The King James Bible), the rights in which
are vested in the Crown, are reproduced by permission of the Crown's Patentee, Cambridge
University Press.

Scripture quotations marked ESV are from the Holy Bible, English Standard Version, published
by HarperCollins Publishers, © 2001 Crossway Bibles, a division of Good News Publishers.
Used by permission. All rights reserved.

Scripture quotations taken from the New American Standard Bible, copyright © 1960, 1962,
1963, 1968, 1971, 1972, 1973, 1975, 1977, 1995 by The Lockman Foundation. Used by
permission.

Scripture taken from the New Century Version. Copyright © 2005 by Thomas Nelson, Inc. Used
by permission. All rights reserved.

A catalogue record for this book is available from the British Library

Printed in Singapore by Craft Print International Ltd

Giving it up

Maggi Dawn

Daily Bible readings from Ash Wednesday to Easter Day

My thanks to my editors at BRF, to my many friends for their constant encouragement, and to Dr Caroline Ramsey, the Revd Henry Martin, the Revd Kathryn Fleming and Danielle Tumminio, without whose patient reading of drafts this book would never have been completed.

Dedicated to my son Benedict,
the greatest of God's blessings to me.

Contents

Introduction

*The real voyage of discovery consists not in seeking new
landscapes but in having new eyes.*

MARCEL PROUST

Of all the traditions associated with Lent, probably the best-
known is the practice of giving something up for the six and a
half weeks from Ash Wednesday to Easter Sunday. The most
common things people give up are chocolate, alcohol, coffee
and sweets. Some people give up something non-edible—a
time-consuming habit, for instance, like watching TV or surfing
the net—and some take the opportunity of Lent to kick a
habit like smoking or swearing. But why do we give things
up? Where did the tradition begin, and what is it supposed to
achieve?

There's clear evidence that for at least 1500 years the Church
has kept a period of fasting during the weeks before Easter,
and it's thought that it may date even further back to the very
early Church. The word 'Lent' comes from the Anglo-Saxon
word *Lencten,* from which we get our word 'lengthen', and it
referred simply to the fact that the weeks leading up to Easter
were the early spring days that were lengthening after the
winter solstice. The oldest traditions of Lent are interwoven
with the idea of spring. Greek Orthodox communities treat
the first day of Lent as a celebration of the first outdoor day of
the new year: spring is the beginning of new life after the death
that came with winter, and so we should go outside to greet it.

In medieval Europe, fasting and abstinence were not restricted to Lent. Eating meat was prohibited by the Church at least one day in every week of the year, and Friday continued to be a 'fish day' until late into the 20th century, as a reminder that it was on Friday that Christ died. In addition to Friday, there were often two or three more days of abstinence in the week, with a great deal of local variation. For instance, in some areas Wednesday was a meat-free day to remember the treason of Judas Iscariot; Saturday was a day to honour the Virgin Mary. There was also a cycle of fasting through the year— the four Ember Days, which mark the beginning of the new seasons, and Advent (the four weeks before Christmas) as well as Lent. So, for the medieval Christian, meat was prohibited for somewhere between a third and a half of all the days in the year; but the Lent fast, representing the 40 days during which Jesus withdrew into the wilderness, was the toughest.

This fast has several purposes. It's supposed to remind us daily that we depend upon God for everything, to draw us closer to God in prayer, to reconnect us to the idea of community, and to help us follow Christ's journey through the wilderness and on to Jerusalem. It's all too easy, though, simply to give up some treat or other for the duration of Lent, feel pleased with ourselves for breaking a bad habit or losing a little weight (or feel a little guilty at not keeping our resolution!) and not really engage with the deeper meaning of Lent.

In the Old Testament, the prophets called the people of God to a 'true fast', one that was not merely the observance of traditions but one that transformed their lives. As we walk through Lent this year, we can explore the idea that there is another kind of 'giving up' that we could do. If we're to draw closer to God, we need to be willing to give up some of our entrenched ideas about God in order to see him more clearly. It's not so much giving up 'false gods'; it's more about identifying false or blurred images of God that have been picked up from the surrounding culture or from our imagination, and allowing them to be replaced. We need to allow the light to be shed on those places where our idea of God is too harsh, too weak, too small, too fragile, too stern.

We'll begin this Lent journey, then, by looking at the traditions of Lent to gain a clearer picture of what they are for, and what biblical imagery they reflect. Then we'll see what Jesus said about fasting and what he gave up when he fasted in the wilderness. We'll look at the way some Old Testament characters traded in their old idea of God for a true encounter, and see how different the real God was from their expectations. Then we'll see how Jesus turned people's ideas about God upside down. Finally, in Holy Week we'll follow some of the events of the last week in Jesus' life, and discover how different he was from the Messiah people were expecting. In the process, we may find that our own preconceived notions of what God 'ought' to be like come in for some re-examination.

This Lent, then, whether or not you're giving up chocolate or anything else, I invite you to take a journey with me through biblical tales of fasts and wildernesses to seek a clearer vision of God. As we travel, let's pray for grace to be flexible enough in our thinking to allow God to reveal himself to us. As I've been writing this book, I've been surprised at the way in which my own ideas have been changed all over again. To see God more clearly almost certainly means being surprised at what we discover.

Let's take the prayer of St Richard of Chichester (1197–1253) as our daily prayer:

Thanks be to thee, my Lord Jesus Christ,
For all the benefits thou hast won for me,
For all the pains and insults thou hast borne for me.

O most merciful Redeemer, Friend, and Brother,
May I know thee more clearly,
Love thee more dearly,
And follow thee more nearly,
Day by day.

Giving up

To dust you shall return

The Lord is merciful and gracious, slow to anger and abounding in steadfast love. He will not always accuse, nor will he keep his anger for ever. He does not deal with us according to our sins, nor repay us according to our iniquities. For as the heavens are high above the earth, so great is his steadfast love towards those who fear him; as far as the east is from the west, so far he removes our transgressions from us. As a father has compassion for his children, so the Lord has compassion for those who fear him. For he knows how we were made; he remembers that we are dust. As for mortals, their days are like grass; they flourish like a flower of the field; for the wind passes over it, and it is gone, and its place knows it no more. But the steadfast love of the Lord is from everlasting to everlasting on those who fear him, and his righteousness to children's children, to those who keep his covenant and remember to do his commandments.

PSALM 103:8–18

I have mixed feelings about the Ash Wednesday liturgy. The ashes from which Ash Wednesday gets its name are made by taking palm crosses from the previous year's Palm Sunday and burning them. During a service of Holy Communion, the fine grey ash is mixed with a little oil and pressed in the shape of the cross on to the forehead of each worshipper with these words: 'Remember that you are but dust: from dust you came, and to dust you shall return. Turn from sin and be faithful to Christ' (see Genesis 3:19). The ashing ritual is a symbol of the fact that we are quite literally made of dust—billion-year-old carbon from burnt-out stars, as Joni Mitchell sang in the 1970s.

Lent is in part about the recognition of our own humanity, but the words 'dust to dust' put us squarely in the same territory as a funeral service. They can seem a dour and punishing declaration of sinfulness, making it hard to see the overriding sense of redemption that the gospel should always carry. Acknowledging both the sinful nature of humanity and our own particular flaws may be essential if we're to escape the arrogance that makes the human heart leaden and ugly, but there's a fine line between that and an over-emphasis on sinfulness, which so easily transforms the lightness of the gospel into the straitjacket of religiosity. How can ashes be, in any sense of the word, redemptive and light?

I think, though, that a lightness does emerge from the process of facing down our own demons. When we look our mortality in the face, the inevitability of our own death asks of us, 'What are you going to do with the life you have?' Years ago I attended the funeral of Steve Fairnie (known to all his friends simply as 'Fairnie'), a remarkable and talented man who died suddenly and unexpectedly. I was unprepared for the blow, not only of losing a friend but of facing the fact that young people—people like me—could just be gone from this world, overnight and without warning. The shock of his death was intensified by the sharp realisation that my own life was far more fragile than I had thought, and the resulting mix of grief and disbelief left me feeling in a slightly dream-like state for some weeks to come. 'I don't think I'm ready for this,' I wrote in the words of a song; 'the thread I'm holding on to is thin.

Would somebody please wake me up? It feels like I'm living in a dream. I don't want to believe that it's true—it's all over.'

The huge church where Fairnie's funeral was held was packed with maybe a thousand people or more—groups of friends and colleagues from widely different contexts—and it gradually became apparent that many of them knew him within their own world without having any idea of the breadth of his influence elsewhere. His art students were there, as were a number of high-profile members of the music industry; there were leading members of various denominations and large contingents from various Christian festivals and communities to which he'd contributed. In place of a traditional sermon, there were tributes and eulogies given by people who had known him in these different contexts, and all over the church you could see people's faces lighting up as they registered the extent of his gifts and achievements. After the funeral was over, tea was served by a group of women from the church, and one of them confided to me, 'We had no idea that he knew all these people. We just thought of him as the college teacher from around the corner.'

In the midst of grief, it seemed that one of Fairnie's parting gifts to his friends was the realisation that we had no idea how long we had to live, either. All the things I'd thought I might do one day suddenly seemed a little more urgent. Not only that, but the breadth of his interests seemed to give permission to flout the cultural wisdom that you can only really do one thing. That day I consciously picked up his Renaissance attitude to life and decided that if I couldn't decide between theology and art and music, then perhaps I would just do them all. Later that year I went to university to take the degree I'd never taken, made another album in my spare time, started writing books and articles, and just for fun I began painting again—something I'd let lie dormant for years.

Despite his many gifts, though, Fairnie wasn't solely focused on achieving things. He always had time for people. I can't count the times he would just stop for a ten-minute chat, and he knew how to get under the skin of a situation enough to find out what was really going on. He always left you feeling six inches taller, and infinitely more capable of living your life. Knowing him left me with the certainty that life can be full, that you should find out what you're good at and do it as much as you can, but also that life is about the community you build, not about building your personal empire.

Pausing to contemplate our mortality on Ash Wednesday is not for the sake of making us bleak, but to startle us into an awareness of the gift of life. We're neither perfect nor immortal: we are merely and yet wonderfully human, and we need to know who we are in our imperfections as well as our gifts in order to live every day as if it counts for something. The call to repentance isn't supposed to leave us dour or morbidly obsessed with our failings. Instead, it's a call to turn away decisively from what keeps us from God, alienates us from other people and stops us from living well. Lent begins with a challenge to clear out the mental and spiritual clutter and so discover how to live life to the full.

A true fast

Is not this the fast that I choose: to loose the bonds of injustice, to undo the thongs of the yoke, to let the oppressed go free, and to break every yoke? Is it not to share your bread with the hungry, and bring the homeless poor into your house; when you see the naked, to cover them, and not to hide yourself from your own kin? Then your light shall break forth like the dawn, and your healing shall spring up quickly; your vindicator shall go before you, the glory of the Lord shall be your rearguard. Then you shall call, and the Lord will answer; you shall cry for help, and he will say, Here I am. If you remove the yoke from among you, the pointing of the finger, the speaking of evil, if you offer your food to the hungry and satisfy the needs of the afflicted, then your light shall rise in the darkness and your gloom be like the noonday. The Lord will guide you continually, and satisfy your needs in parched places, and make your bones strong; and you shall be like a watered garden, like a spring of water, whose waters never fail. Your ancient ruins shall be rebuilt; you shall raise up the foundations of many generations; you shall be called the repairer of the breach, the restorer of streets to live in.

ISAIAH 58:6–12

In most parts of Europe, the day before Lent is celebrated with some kind of feast or carnival. In England it's called

Shrove Tuesday, the word 'shrove' coming from the same root as 'shrive' or 'shriven', a Middle English word meaning to absolve after hearing confession. In French cultures the day before Lent is called *Mardi Gras* (literally, 'Fat Tuesday'), which has become synonymous with the idea of party and carnival, a time for relishing freedom and plenty before the fast begins. The Mardi Gras carnival has become almost entirely separated from Lent, featuring more as a stand-alone feast than a precursor to the period of discipline and self-restraint that is supposed to follow. It's interesting, too, to see that Shrove Tuesday is now more commonly known by its popular name, Pancake Day, and, like Mardi Gras, has begun to emerge as a non-religious feast.

One day last year, I was standing in a supermarket check-out queue when the woman in front of me suddenly exclaimed, 'I forgot to buy a lemon!' She sent one of her children back to get one and, while she was apologising to me for holding up the queue, she explained that she had realised only at the last moment that it was Pancake Day, so she had rushed to the shops specially to buy eggs, sugar, flour, butter and syrup to make their pancakes. We swapped opinions as to whether or not you get better pancakes if you let your pancake batter stand for an hour before you cook it. And then I asked her whether she knew that Pancake Day was the day before Lent. 'Lent?' she said quizzically. 'What's that, then?'

A few hundred years ago, people would have been baffled if they'd been told that anybody would rush out to buy extra food to celebrate Pancake Day, since the whole point of the pancakes was to use up all the remaining foods that were forbidden during Lent. We know from medieval recipe books that all meat and dairy products were given up for Lent. Households would gradually run down their supplies as Lent approached so that they didn't go to waste once Lent began, and on the evening of Shrove Tuesday all remaining eggs, milk, butter and animal fats were used up in the pancake feast.

We seem to be far better at feasting than fasting in our society; but it's interesting that Isaiah seems to suggest that obeying religious rules about what we eat and drink is, in the end, of little interest to God. The 'true fast' that the prophets called for meant not just observing religious rituals but changing the way people lived. Isaiah says that what God really cares about is justice, generosity, and caring for the poor and the weak.

If fasting is merely a display of personal self-discipline, then it is a declaration of one's ability to be spiritual without any help from God. To become the kind of people Isaiah describes, we need an inner transformation that we can't achieve by our own efforts. It doesn't happen through the fasting itself; only God can transform our souls.

So is there any point in fasting at all? Should we abandon the practice of giving things up, and instead attend simply to the issues that Isaiah names, like fighting against injustice and oppression? Even though these are the issues that really matter, there is still value in giving things up for a time, simply because it pushes us to be countercultural. We live in a society that eats, drinks and spends to excess, and even in recessionary times we have more than most of the world can dream of. Much of what we buy, we do not use. Research published in March 2007 revealed that about one-third of food bought in British shops ends up in rubbish bins. The Waste and Resources Action Programme (WRAP), a government body funded by Defra, said that overbuying, wrong storage temperatures and fussy children were among the reasons people gave for throwing away 6.7 million tonnes of food waste a year, only half of which is peelings, scraps and bones. A staggering half of that amount is perfectly edible food that just hasn't been eaten.

Before leaving the memory of Shrove Tuesday behind, it's

sobering to reflect on the fact that Pancake Day, which began as a way of using up surplus food, has now become yet one more opportunity for supermarkets to sell us more and more food, much of which will end up going to waste. One radical move we could make this Lent is to look at the level of waste in our own households. Instead of giving up desserts or coffee, what if we gave up an hour or two each week during Lent to rethink our shopping and cooking habits so that we buy and cook only what we need, use up leftovers and reduce unnecessary waste? Maybe next year, instead of buying extra food that we don't need for Pancake Day, we could return to celebrating it as a feast of leftovers. When we discover that change is possible in our kitchens, we'll begin to believe that it's also possible on a global scale, and that the inequality and injustice in the world really can be addressed.

More than the body

[Jesus] said to his disciples, 'Therefore I tell you, do not worry about your life, what you will eat, or about your body, what you will wear. For life is more than food, and the body more than clothing. Consider the ravens: they neither sow nor reap, they have neither storehouse nor barn, and yet God feeds them. Of how much more value are you than the birds! And can any of you by worrying add a single hour to your span of life? If then you are not able to do so small a thing as that, why do you worry about the rest? Consider the lilies, how they grow: they neither toil nor spin; yet I tell you, even Solomon in all his glory was not clothed like one of these. But if God so clothes the grass of the field, which is alive today and tomorrow is thrown into the oven, how much more will he clothe you—you of little faith! And do not keep striving for what you are to eat and what you are to drink, and do not keep worrying. For it is the nations of the world that strive after all these things, and your Father knows that you need them. Instead, strive for his kingdom, and these things will be given to you as well.

'Do not be afraid, little flock, for it is your Father's good pleasure to give you the kingdom. Sell your possessions, and give alms. Make purses for yourselves that do not wear out, an unfailing treasure in heaven, where no thief comes near and no moth destroys. For where your treasure is, there your heart will be also.'

LUKE 12:22–34

I remember, a few years back, reading a column in one of the national newspapers in which the commentator wrote dismissively of the whole idea of Lent, saying that he didn't see why giving things up should earn God's forgiveness of our personal failings. In fact, without realising it, he hit the nail on the head! Giving things up for Lent has never been about earning anything from God, least of all forgiveness. Christianity is founded on the idea that we *cannot* atone, or make payment, for our wrongdoings. The whole point of the gospel is that we cannot save ourselves or buy or earn God's love or forgiveness through self-sacrifice.

It's perhaps no surprise, if people believe God is such a hard taskmaster, that they want to keep their distance from religion. But a God who demands that we earn our forgiveness is very far indeed from the Christian concept of God. We don't have to read far into the New Testament to find Jesus teaching that God is not harsh or legalistic, but full of grace and goodness. Yet it seems to be a human tendency to believe that a joyless, judgmental God who demands endless penance is more suitable to a religious disposition. Maybe we cannot cope with a God who is joy-giving, generous, forgiving and the giver of all good gifts. The negative effect of the tendency to replace a life-giving God with a dark and lifeless religion has a venerable history, and the habit of turning Lent from an exercise in drawing close to God into a self-punishing stoicism is a case in point.

The traditional Lenten fast was exclusively to do with food and drink, not about giving up bad habits—and it wasn't only about giving up luxuries such as chocolate or coffee, but everyday essentials. Not only was meat prohibited but everything that was of animal origin, including milk, butter, cheese and eggs. To make matters even more difficult, as Lent fell at the end of winter, supplies of other foods were fairly slim. It's hard for us to imagine now, with our ready availability of imported fruit and vegetables. In generations gone by, what was left of fruit and vegetables by February would mostly be old and wrinkled, and possibly a bit mouldy. Only cabbages and winter leeks would be fresh. Lent would have been spent eating mostly bread, porridge, peas or beans, salted or dried vegetables, fish (fresh or preserved), onions, leeks and rather old apples, unless you were wealthy, in which case you might also have had a few dried dates, figs, raisins and almonds.

The Lenten fast, then, was focused on giving up the daily essentials of life. Statements such as 'life is more than food', and 'man shall not live by bread alone' (Matthew 4:4, RSV) had a chance to become a daily reality when the community deprived itself of its regular diet.

Lent is not about earning forgiveness, but neither is it about achieving our aspirations. At a physical level, we seem prone to turning Lent into an exercise in self-improvement. A couple of years back, someone said to me, 'It's a good thing Lent is nearly here. I need to lose some weight, and I like the fact that Lent imposes a timescale and a deadline to achieve that.' Another told me, 'Giving something up is good because it stops you spending too much on stuff you don't need.' Both of these views are based on the misconception that Lent is about giving up things that are bad for us, like smoking or overeating or buying too many consumer goods. Originally, Lent was about giving up things that are *good* for us, essentials rather than luxuries, not for therapy or self-improvement but to reconnect our understanding of our daily existence to God. Even though a cycle of moderate fasting and feasting is undeniably good for the body as well as the soul, the meaning of Lent is lost if it gets subsumed into the quest for a perfect body or a regime of fitness.

In a society obsessed with the body beautiful, it's all too easy to slip into the idea that fasting is focused on the individual. Somehow, a half-remembered custom of giving things up has been mixed into our society's obsession with self-help and self-improvement. As a result, we've blurred the true meaning of the fast into a rather individualistic concept, like a New Year resolution to detox or declutter.

Fasting in the Christian tradition is essentially about recognising that there's nothing we *can* do to improve ourselves. We are fallen creatures and need redemption, not cosmetic surgery. No amount of self-improvement will change God's view of us—God, who knows us better than we know ourselves, who is not fooled by the way we present ourselves in prayer or religious observance, and who loves us anyway. We do not need to put on a show for him and we cannot save ourselves apart from him. We are not trying to impress God or the person next to us; neither should we be trying to impress ourselves, satisfying our egos with the idea that we are very cool, very smart and very in control. The point of the fast is, in fact, to humble ourselves—an old-fashioned word that really means accepting with absolute honesty our true self, in terms of both good points and bad.

Lent, then, is not about giving up luxuries or losing weight, not about food per se, not about decluttering or feng shui or any other kind of feel-good, detoxifying exercise. If fasting allows us the space to face reality and gaze more deeply into the honest yet loving face of God, it's worth working at. But if we regard the Lenten fast as an opportunity to lose weight, improve our skin tone or drop a size in clothes, we'll miss the point altogether.

In the end, Lent is about denying ourselves some of the essentials of everyday life in order to focus on the reality that we depend upon God for life itself. It's about realigning ourselves with God and his purposes in our world; about reminding ourselves that all we have is a gift from God in any case. If our Lenten fast is understood well, it will relieve us of the need to try harder, achieve more, feel more worthy. It will ground us in the firm and unshakeable knowledge that we are human— we are but dust, and to dust we shall return—but that to be human is enough, under the loving gaze of God.

What does the Lord require?

Hear what the Lord says: Rise, plead your case before the mountains, and let the hills hear your voice. Hear, you mountains, the controversy of the Lord, and you enduring foundations of the earth; for the Lord has a controversy with his people, and he will contend with Israel.

'O my people, what have I done to you? In what have I wearied you? Answer me! For I brought you up from the land of Egypt, and redeemed you from the house of slavery; and I sent before you Moses, Aaron, and Miriam. O my people, remember now what King Balak of Moab devised, what Balaam son of Beor answered him, and what happened from Shittim to Gilgal, that you may know the saving acts of the Lord.'

'With what shall I come before the Lord, and bow myself before God on high? Shall I come before him with burnt-offerings, with calves a year old? Will the Lord be pleased with thousands of rams, with tens of thousands of rivers of oil? Shall I give my firstborn for my transgression, the fruit of my body for the sin of my soul?'

He has told you, O mortal, what is good; and what does the Lord require of you but to do justice, and to love kindness, and to walk humbly with your God?

MICAH 6:1–8

So, *have* you given up anything for Lent this year? How did you choose what to give up? Did you decide all by yourself or did you consult with anyone else?

We've already considered the way the Lenten fast has evolved over time in several ways, so that now, if people are giving up anything at all, it's often a luxury item such as coffee or chocolate or desserts rather than a daily essential. In addition, it may not be an item of food at all, but something like smoking or watching TV, or people may be following the new trend of taking something up instead of giving something up.

One of the most dramatic changes in the way Lent is observed can be seen in the shift from a community to an individual fast. Today, people usually decide individually what to give up for Lent, which brings the temptation to choose something involving self-improvement. In medieval times, though, as we've already considered, there was no element of personal choice about the Lent fast. The rules were known throughout the community, and everybody did the same.

Changing the way a tradition is practised sooner or later changes its meaning. Giving up luxuries rather than everyday foods has shifted the meaning of Lent away from the idea that we depend on God for life itself. Similarly, when each individual chooses their own style of fast, the idea of Lent as a community event is largely lost. This loss is felt in two ways. Firstly, if everyone abides by the same fast, it's easier to do, and there's a sense of the community walking together. There's an automatic accountability: you can't just quietly give up halfway through, hoping no one will notice, and there's a sense in which, if you break your fast, it affects the whole group. When everyone has the same practice, a sense of community is built up.

The traditional, uniform fast also provided a practical way to build up the community, because of its strong association with social justice and the redistribution of wealth. As well as abstaining from certain foods, people were encouraged to fast completely from time to time—for instance, by giving up one whole meal on a given day. The money saved on these occasions would be given (in the days before a welfare state and a National Health Service) towards the charitable aid of the hungry and poor. In this situation, while Lent may start with the idea of withdrawal into the desert to reconnect with God, it ends in a changed relationship to the wider world.

It seems unlikely that we'll ever recover the kind of community-wide fast that was common in medieval times, but it might be possible for churches or church groups to agree on a common Lenten discipline, or to meet for a communal 'poverty' supper from which proceeds and donations are given to charity. Remaining accountable to a group enhances the sense of common purpose and helps to focus the fast on drawing close to God and to one another, reminding us that we're part of the human race. It also makes real in everyday life the fact that our relationship to God is not privatised. Our faith affects our relationship to the world.

What does the Lord require of us? As in the days of Micah, forgiveness is not earnt through self-sacrifice, and holiness is not achieved through discipline or public shows of generosity. Theologically speaking, forgiveness and holiness are gifts from God, not things that we earn or achieve. As James pointed out in his epistle, though, to say we love God and then do nothing for those in need makes a mockery of our faith (James 2:16). To do justice and to love kindness turns our focus outwards towards the community. Finding a way of keeping Lent together as a community, and for the community, reminds us every day that the earth is the Lord's and everything in it (Psalm 24:1); that all good things, even life itself, are gifts from God (James 1:17) and that we are not here solely to take care of our own interests but to serve one another in the love of Christ. If Lent needs to be realised not as an individualistic journey but as a community exercise, how can we make use of Lenten disciplines to develop that recognition?

We live in a world where countless people are homeless, hungry or living in poverty—a world where 40 per cent of the world's wealth is owned by one per cent of its people. It may be simplistic to think that the tiny difference we would make by reducing our own wasteful lives and giving to charity would be anything more than a drop in the ocean. But if we don't begin by examining our own lives, we don't even have a foot on the ladder of change. We may not be able to do everything but we can do something rather than nothing. We can't bring inequality to an end from our own kitchen, but we can begin there.

Questions for reflection

- 'Remember that you are but dust.' Life is a gift: how can we live it to the full? What do we mean to do with our lives? What is stopping us?
- 'We need redemption, not cosmetic surgery.' If God both knows and loves me, what do I need to accept about myself?
- What does the Lord require of us? How can we keep Lent in a way that serves the community rather than improving ourselves?

Jesus in the wilderness and beyond

Old and new

Then they said to him, 'John's disciples, like the disciples of the Pharisees, frequently fast and pray, but your disciples eat and drink.' Jesus said to them, 'You cannot make wedding-guests fast while the bridegroom is with them, can you? The days will come when the bridegroom will be taken away from them, and then they will fast in those days.' He also told them a parable: 'No one tears a piece from a new garment and sews it on an old garment; otherwise the new will be torn, and the piece from the new will not match the old. And no one puts new wine into old wineskins; otherwise the new wine will burst the skins and will be spilled, and the skins will be destroyed. But new wine must be put into fresh wineskins. And no one after drinking old wine desires new wine, but says, "The old is good."'

LUKE 5:33–39

Fasting was a common religious practice in the first century, with many Jews fasting ritually twice a week. The one great fast ordained in the Old Testament was the fast on the Day of Atonement (Leviticus 16:29–31), but Jews also called fasts on special occasions, such as when they went to war (Judges 20:26), when loved ones were ill (2 Samuel 12:16–23), when someone died (1 Samuel 31:13; 2 Samuel 1:12), when they needed forgiveness (Deuteronomy 9:15–18; 1 Kings

21:17–29), when they were faced with trouble or danger (2 Chronicles 20:3; Nehemiah 1:4), and at difficult or significant moments in their lives (Esther 4:16).

Although Jesus was so visibly effective in public ministry, he didn't seem to practise ritual fasting in the same way that others did, and neither did his disciples. This is not to say that Jesus never fasted, as we shall see when we read the story of his long fast in the wilderness, but he didn't fast as regularly or publicly as the Pharisees or John the Baptist and his disciples. It's unclear from today's story whether Jesus' interlocutors were offended or intrigued by this, but they wanted to know why he didn't observe the accepted conventions.

Their question is direct enough: why are you doing things differently from the accepted traditional way? But Jesus' parables usually give an oblique answer to a question, taking the discussion off in another direction. This one is no exception and is both intriguing and frustrating in its failure to answer the question directly, instead picking up the issue of following long-held traditions. It's almost as if Jesus is saying, 'I'll give you an answer, but first I need to point out that you're asking the wrong question…'

If we were to interpret the parable of the wineskins as a direct answer to the question, we might take Jesus' words as a divine mandate to abandon ancient liturgies and institutional structures in favour of new forms of spirituality, new ways of being Church. But a closer look reveals that the parable doesn't praise innovation over tradition; nor does it reject what is old. Jesus uses the metaphor of wine-making to show that new things are important but that old and new things don't mix easily. Then he gives a twist to the tale by saying that usually the old wine tastes better. So what are we to do with the parable of the wineskins? How are we to apply Jesus' words to our own negotiations of old and new ways of doing things?

Debates arise regularly about new directions in the life of the Church. There are arguments about what kind of music we have, what kind of liturgy, what kind of church order and hierarchy and leadership, what interpretation of theology, how we read and interpret the Bible. There have always been those who have argued that new is better than old and that to follow Jesus means rejecting old traditions, leaving behind outdated language and the baggage of institutional structures. On the other hand, there have always been others who have argued that faithfulness to tradition is the only way to maintain truth and authenticity.

What I like about the parable of the wineskins is that the production of wine is an organic process. Too often, arguments about maintaining or changing tradition fall into the trap of assuming that tradition itself is static, and fail to acknowledge that it actually changes all the time, both in practice and meaning. As with a wine maturing in a cellar, the change may be so gradual that it's invisible from one day to the next, but a good vintner knows from experience that the wine is continuing to develop, and will be able to make an educated guess as to when it will be at its best.

Is new wine always better, then? If you have ever drunk good wine, you'll know different. Given the choice, a good quality, well-aged wine is always going to be better than a young one. For everyday purposes, there are some wines that do not improve with age—they are for the moment—but it's also true that to have good wine ready in ten years' time, you have to be making it now. A wine drunk too soon or not stored properly will always taste inferior. The skill lies in knowing which wine is which: which ones to drink young, which ones to store, and when to bring out the old stuff to its best advantage.

As with wine, so with church. Jesus' words don't praise old over new, or new over old; they show that old and new must coexist. There are times when the need is for fresh and young experiments. Who would have thought that growing wine at high altitude in South America would ever be worthwhile? It took a visionary winemaker to try the experiment, someone stubborn enough to ignore those who assured him he was wasting his time, and patient enough to endure a few bad years before the technique produced a rare and beautiful wine. Who would have thought that meeting in a pub on a Tuesday night, or creating events in parks or beaches on a Saturday, could be a legitimate way of being church? Yet that is exactly what is happening all over the UK, and whether these activities will prove as ephemeral as young wines, only time will tell. Experimental ways of doing church need vision, they need enough space and freedom to be different, and they need enough time to try and fail a few times until a good mix emerges.

This doesn't mean, though, that the old ways of doing and being church are over. Like old wine, there is a quality to what has been tried and tested and given ample time to mature. The process of maturing wine changes the shape and nature of the containers holding it, and these containers need to be treated with respect and care, or the acidity and sharpness of the new wine will burst the mature skins. The same goes for church.

We need what is new and fresh and of-the-moment in church, and we need the old, rich, high-quality traditions. We also need to develop a nose for new things that are worth maturing and keeping: after all, if there is to be vintage wine in the future, it has to be made now. And when an experiment has really gone sour, we need the courage to put it aside without wasting too much time on sentimentality or regret.

When the appeal to tradition is used to try to press new ideas into old formats or to make the new seem as comfortable and conventional as the old, the two interact badly and both old and new get spoilt and wasted. So let the old be good at being what it is! If it has matured into something glorious, you don't need to improve it; you just need to allow it to be, like a vintage wine. At the same time, we need to create new things, enjoy what is young and fresh, and develop a nose for what can be left to mature for future generations.

Stones into bread

Then Jesus was led up by the Spirit into the wilderness to be tempted by the devil. He fasted for forty days and forty nights, and afterwards he was famished. The tempter came and said to him, 'If you are the Son of God, command these stones to become loaves of bread.' But he answered, 'It is written, "One does not live by bread alone, but by every word that comes from the mouth of God."'

MATTHEW 4:1–4

From yesterday's reading, we know that Jesus and his disciples didn't keep all the ritual fasts of his time, but as we can see from this famous story of his temptations in the wilderness, there were times when he did fast.

It's unlikely that this fast was literally 40 days long. Forty days is used symbolically throughout the biblical accounts to indicate a period of preparation and transformation. Noah's life was transformed first by 40 days of rain (Genesis 7:12), and then by 40 days of waiting as his ark rested on Ararat before he sent out a raven to search for dry land (8:6). Moses prayed for 40-day periods on Mount Sinai (Exodus 24:18; 34:28; Deuteronomy 9:7–29), the spies spent 40 days scouting out the promised land (Numbers 13:25), and Elijah travelled 40 days on the strength given him by the meal that an angel brought him (1 Kings 19:8). David was prepared for kingship through a 40-day challenge issued by Goliath

(1 Samuel 17:16) and, when God sent Jonah to Nineveh, the city was given a period of 40 days to change its ways (Jonah 3:4). Here, then, describing Jesus' fast as lasting 40 days indicates its importance as a period of preparation and transformation before embarking on his public ministry and his eventual journey to Jerusalem.

The symbolism of 40 days as a time of preparation helps to interpret the purpose of Jesus' wilderness fast. The three Synoptic Gospels, Matthew, Mark and Luke, place this fast immediately after Jesus' baptism by John, when the Spirit descended on him and God's voice identified him as his Son. We don't really know whether Jesus always knew deep down that he was the Messiah or whether his sense of his identity and calling evolved in him gradually. Either way, the baptism was clearly a crystallising moment: when Jesus saw the heavens opened and the dove resting on him, and heard God's voice, he knew his identity and calling without doubt, and also knew that it was time to begin his public ministry.

As Jesus contemplated his ministry, he must have been aware of the seriousness and the potential dangers of the task of proclaiming the kingdom of God. The fast focused his attention on his priorities and on the great temptations that come to anyone involved in ministry or public service.

Jesus' temptations show us that he really was human—not just God in a human mask but real flesh and blood. It hurt when he got a splinter, he knew what it was like to fall in love, and when his friends let him down it was as devastating for him as it is for you and me. These stories sum up in three episodes every major kind of temptation that you or I have to deal with. The first temptation concerned food itself—hunger and perhaps, by extension, other physical appetites, too. Jesus recognised that he could use his gifts and power simply to serve his own desires, but his reply to that temptation, 'One does not live by bread alone', serves as a dual reminder. On the one hand, life is about more than physical appetites and desires, more than the daily round of earning, cooking, eating and sleeping. Christian belief continues to claim that life has a meaning and purpose beyond its physical and material aspects.

On the other hand, placing these words in the context of an actual physical fast reminds us, by picturing the sheer difficulty of enduring self-discipline, that we can't transcend our physicality. Some of the early heresies that were rejected by Christianity were based on dualistic ideas of Greek and Persian origins, which held that the spirit was superior to the body and that the body must be sublimated. Undeniably, Christian thought has soaked up some of this dualism through the centuries and has frequently expressed an uncomfortable relationship between spirituality and physicality. Yet the heart of Christianity is the incarnation of Jesus, the God-made-man, which places the emphasis squarely on the wholeness and unity of human existence. We are not spirits clothed inconveniently in bodies; rather, we are bodily creatures.

One of the purposes of the Lenten fast is to remind us daily that we are physical creatures and live a physical existence. In a society that is both overindulgent and excessively body-conscious, perhaps one of the challenges of Lent is to befriend our own bodies and find a good balance between taking care of ourselves and simply living comfortably in our own skins. At the same time, Lent reminds us that we are more than mere animals: we have spiritual and moral capabilities. We are governed not only by our appetites and needs but also by our will and our imagination.

Fame and fortune

Then the devil led Jesus to the holy city of Jerusalem and put
him on a high place of the Temple. The devil said, 'If you
are the Son of God, jump down, because it is written in the
Scriptures: "He has put his angels in charge of you. They will
catch you in their hands so that you will not hit your foot on
a rock."' Jesus answered him, 'It also says in the Scriptures,
"Do not test the Lord your God."'

MATTHEW 4:5–7 (NCV)

Marjoe Gortner was a talented child, born in 1943 to parents
who were evangelists in a Pentecostal denomination in Cali-
fornia. His unusual name was a contraction of Mary and
Joseph, and early in his life his parents spotted his potential
as a child preacher. At the age of three he was ordained, and at
four he presided over a wedding for the first time (something
that threw Californian lawyers into a bit of a spin over the
validity of the marriage!). For the next ten years, his parents
toured Marjoe the child preacher around independent Pentecostal churches and tent meetings in the American South
and Midwest, where he was lauded as a miraculous example
of divine inspiration as the voice of God seemingly spoke
through a young child. In his teens he vanished from the
preaching circuit for a number of years, but as an adult he
resumed his ministry, once again amazing audiences with
his ability to hear God's voice concerning the illnesses and

troubles of people in the audiences, calling them forward for prayers of healing.

Years later, in 1972, Marjoe appeared in a documentary about his own life, confessing onscreen to the truth behind his ministry. He claimed that, as a child, he had been carefully coached by his parents, under extreme discipline, to learn his lines and the techniques of his childhood ministry, which brought in a large income for his parents through donations from the audiences. At the age of 14, he fled the life of ministry and lived for some years with an older woman, while he first caught up on his education and then tried a series of unsuccessful careers. Later he returned to preaching, apparently hoping at the outset to preach with integrity about personal transformation and a God of justice. But he discovered that a ministry of integrity brought neither the fame nor the large income that his earlier, extraordinary antics had done. Whether through personal weakness or through the pressure to give his audiences the kind of revivalism they craved, he began using the skills he'd learnt as a child to build the crowds up into a religious frenzy, creating an illusion of spiritual ministry that was, in the end, nothing more than mass hysteria. Once again he made a large income from this 'ministry', but eventually gave it up for good.

Gortner agreed to make the 1972 documentary to show that what he called 'the religion business' was a complete con, and to reveal the techniques he and his team used to create the impression that he was hearing from God. It's said that truth is stranger than fiction: Steve Martin in *Leap of Faith* (1992), a fictional comedy about a charlatan preacher and healer, seems quite moderate and sane by comparison to the real-life story told by Marjoe. Once the film of his life was released, it's said that Gortner received a number of death threats from those for whom 'the religion business' was a way of life. Did they want to defend their integrity or just their livelihood? Who knows? Only God can read the heart.

Spiritual gifts can quickly draw a lot of attention, which needs handling carefully if it is not simply to feed the ego of the minister and be used for personal gain. It seems, from the number of ministries that do go awry, that it's entirely possible to use spiritual gifts to gain a lifestyle elevated above the realities of ordinary life. Some people achieve it on a grand international scale, while others simply create a comfortable but not quite real existence for themselves within a small community.

One of the sad results of this particular temptation is the muddling of real ministry with a selfish motivation, so that others often become deceived by the promise of miracles and healings. But perhaps the saddest aspect is that, often, spiritual leaders deceive themselves even more than they deceive others. Wanting to appear more holy and spiritual than everyone else can be really tempting but, just like jumping off high buildings, it does you serious damage when you hit the ground. Like Jesus, we need to be realistic in our view of ourselves and in the way we present ourselves to others. The only way we can truly serve God is if we do so without seeking personal status or glory; a self-seeking 'ministry' is by definition not a ministry at all.

Is this temptation reserved only for professional ministers, then—those who are paid and titled for their work? I would say not. Whether televised and of international note or on a small local scale, gifts of a spiritual nature can be utilised both within recognised church structures and also in a totally maverick fashion. The temptation is there, for anyone who is interested in spiritual things, to take advantage of spirituality for their own comfort. Undoubtedly, though, those who are unusually gifted and become publicly renowned in ministry are especially vulnerable to this kind of temptation. As a church, we need to take care of our own ministers, by praying for them and holding them accountable, but also by ensuring that we don't put them on the pedestals that subject them to such pressure in the first place. The more we heap adulation on those who are great preachers or healers or guides, the more we collaborate in subjecting them to temptation. The greatest favour we can do for those with outstanding spiritual gifts is to resist the tendency to worship them, and instead treat them like ordinary human beings.

Power and glory

Then the devil led Jesus to the top of a very high mountain and showed him all the kingdoms of the world and all their splendour. The devil said, 'If you will bow down and worship me, I will give you all these things.' Jesus said to the devil, 'Go away from me, Satan! It is written in the Scriptures, "You must worship the Lord your God and serve only him."' So the devil left Jesus, and angels came and took care of him.
MATTHEW 4:8–11 (NCV)

This is the third and final temptation that Jesus encountered in the wilderness and, like the second temptation, it has to do with power. Here, though, I think the temptation is to use religious power not for personal fame and fortune but to gain political or social power—power over people, situations or institutions. It could be for personal gain or for the sheer ego-trip of being in control, but in a way it's a more subtle temptation than the second because we can't do much at all without engaging with the use of power.

Misusing power to take control is a temptation that comes to all of us in some way or another. Not everyone wants to rule the world but most people at least want to control their own little world. Even the desire to maintain a small, private, untroubled realm is, in the end, the desire to be the king of all we survey, even if it's with limited ambitions. But when the human desire for control is mixed with belief in a God of unlimited power, the temptation to abuse power can hit overdrive.

The evidence of God's power in our lives is shown not through controlling other people but through using the power we have to serve others. Look at Jesus, who, the night before he died, took off his coat, put on an apron and washed the dirty feet of his friends (John 13:1–17), a job normally done by the lowest-ranking servant. The most powerful religious person ever to walk the earth showed the love of God through acts of service and self-sacrifice—the very opposite of a control freak. To overcome this temptation, we have to discern between the right use of power, which enables and empowers other people, and the wrong use of power, which simply puts us in charge and denies others their empowerment.

I once worked with someone who told me that the only way to get anything done was by 'the benign use of a little bullying here and there'. It's true that, at times, tough decisions have to be made in order to get anything done, but the manipulative and underhand use of 'benign bullying' is not, I think, what Jesus calls us to. Instead, we need to take up power boldly and transparently and use it for the benefit of others. It takes the self-confidence that comes from genuine humility not to control others but to serve them in the name of God. It's a fine distinction, though, and that's what makes this temptation perhaps the hardest to overcome.

The three temptations that Jesus faced seem to offer short-cuts to what God promises us in any case—to meet our needs, to give us valuable and fulfilled lives, and to enable us to use our gifts for the benefit of the world. The trick of evil is to lure us into shortcuts that give us 15 minutes of fame and a lifetime of regret, but authentic Christianity is a lifetime's task, not a crash course. We need to pace ourselves, keep a clear view of what we're here for, and not give way to the temptation to use our God-given gifts for selfish ends.

No fear

Now when Jesus heard that John had been arrested, he withdrew to Galilee. He left Nazareth and made his home in Capernaum by the lake, in the territory of Zebulun and Naphtali, so that what had been spoken through the prophet Isaiah might be fulfilled:

'Land of Zebulun, land of Naphtali, on the road by the sea, across the Jordan, Galilee of the Gentiles—the people who sat in darkness have seen a great light, and for those who sat in the region and shadow of death light has dawned.'

From that time Jesus began to proclaim, 'Repent, for the kingdom of heaven has come near.'

MATTHEW 4:12–17

John the Baptist was Jesus' older cousin and, although their styles were different, they were both radical preachers who tended to upset the status quo. John resembled the prophets of old, denying himself the comforts of life, living very simply in the wilderness, away from the intensity of life in the town. Perhaps the closest thing we have to John's lifestyle in modern-day Christianity is life in a monastery. As a child, I gained the impression that the monastic life was so separated from ordinary life as to be quite out of touch, but years later, when I first visited a monastery, I discovered that although the monks lived at one remove from the rest of society, in some ways their uncluttered and disciplined life made them able to see more clearly what really matters. John the Baptist was certainly very perceptive about the motivations of the people he met and about the direction of the society on whose fringe he lived. Perhaps that's why, despite his idiosyncracies, people came from miles around to hear him preach and be baptised by him in the River Jordan.

Jesus, on the other hand, lived and worked within a small community and, as he was later accused of being a glutton and a drunkard, he clearly had a lively involvement in everyday life (Luke 7:33–34). Not only that, but when his public ministry began, the neighbours who had at first been impressed with his eloquence (4:22) became outraged when his words seemed to challenge them (vv. 28–29). It's one thing to admire the son of the guy next door when he makes a good start in his career. It's quite another to accept him as a challenging leader.

As the Gospels tell it, baptising Jesus was one of the last things John did before he was imprisoned and executed by Herod. John preached against Herod's adulterous marriage to his brother's wife, Herodias, and for that reason Herodias held a grudge against John and wanted him put to death. At first, Herod protected John: not only did he enjoy listening to John, but to kill him would have been a politically bad move, as Herod's subjects considered John to be a prophet. The historian Josephus records that Herod held John in a fortress called Machaerus, east of the Dead Sea. When Herod celebrated his birthday with a banquet, Herodias called her daughter, Salome, to dance for Herod and his guests. Herod was so pleased that he swore to give her anything she requested, up to half of his kingdom. Salome asked her mother's advice and Herodias grabbed her opportunity, telling Salome to ask for the head of John the Baptist on a plate. Although Herod immediately repented of his offer, because he had made an oath in front of his guests he immediately ordered John's execution (see Mark 6:17–28).

While John had been imprisoned, Jesus must have read the signs and known that his own life would be in danger if he continued with his bold preaching—especially since, as we see here, he began preaching with John's tagline: 'Repent, for the kingdom of heaven has come near.' Perhaps another temptation came to him at this point, as it would to most people who face threats from bullying and power-hungry people—to change his plans, take control of his circumstances and make himself safe. He might have considered whether he should tone down his act or even go underground, in case he too ended up in a prison cell awaiting his own death. He must have weighed up whether to continue or not, or whether he could move elsewhere and fulfil his calling without making himself a willing victim of Herod or anyone else.

One classic response to bullying is to withdraw into yourself; another is to regain control by bullying other people. But Jesus did neither of these: in fact, he did the opposite. His response was one of neither counter-aggression nor shrinking fear. We read that he 'withdrew' and went back to Galilee, which removed him from the scene of John's death. Far from toning down his message or keeping a low profile, though, he chose this moment to expand the scope of his gospel to include not only his own people but the whole world. He went among the Gentiles—the 'outsiders'—to live and preach the good news of the kingdom of God to an even wider audience. So Jesus' first brush with bullies was a real threat to him but he found a way of refusing to become a victim. He moved out of their immediate sight but expanded what he was doing, becoming even more inclusive with his gospel. When we encounter bullying from others, whether because of our faith or other issues, we need to know how to continue in our calling without giving in. It takes wisdom to avoid unnecessary trouble, stubbornness to live our lives regardless of bullies, and enough courage and love to work in contrary flow to the bullying behaviour—including outsiders instead of victimising them.

God's kingdom, as Jesus said, is characterised by light—a metaphor for hope and truth. We have only a simple record here that Jesus 'withdrew' and began to proclaim the kingdom in another part of the country. Reading between the lines, though, we can catch a glimpse of the fact that even early in his ministry Jesus was going against the grain, and that, in order to proclaim the kingdom, he had to work out how to live it. Carrying out his ministry despite living in brutal and dangerous times was one aspect of his strategy. Surviving the tactics of bullies without letting them make our life smaller is really hard work, as I know from experience. But when we emerge on the other side and find that we have discovered the resources to stand our ground, it does feel like the light dawning after darkness.

Follow

As Jesus was walking by Lake Galilee, he saw two brothers, Simon (called Peter) and his brother Andrew. They were throwing a net into the lake because they were fishermen. Jesus said, 'Come follow me, and I will make you fish for people.' So Simon and Andrew immediately left their nets and followed him. As Jesus continued walking by Lake Galilee, he saw two other brothers, James and John, the sons of Zebedee. They were in a boat with their father Zebedee, mending their nets. Jesus told them to come with him. Immediately they left the boat and their father, and they followed Jesus.

MATTHEW 4:18–22 (NCV)

In the early 1990s, when I was earning my living in the music business, I released an album of songs on the theme of following Jesus. The title of the album was *Follow*, and the cover photographer latched on to the connection between the title and the fact that my style of dressing at the time always involved a pair of Doc Martens®. (One of the things to love about grunge was the rare opportunity to wear cool clothes while having perfectly comfortable feet!) I spent an entire day in a photography studio, being photographed from all sorts of angles but always with the boots at the front of the picture. I came away from the shoot not only with good photos for the album but with the idea lodged for ever in my mind that following Jesus means actually putting your feet to the floor and going somewhere.

Whether we follow an individual, a group or an ideal, we should always ask ourselves who we're following and why we do it. We saw earlier this week that Jesus refused the temptation to control people or coerce them into becoming his followers. Instead, he allowed himself to become a servant to those whom he loved. By refusing to be a manipulator, Jesus became the embodiment of an enormously liberating message, and consequently people flocked to follow him.

We can't construct Jesus' personality from the Gospels: they are not biographical accounts and we don't know what he was like as a person, any more than we know what he looked like. From the glimpses we have, though, it appears that he was by turns quite rude and abrupt to some people and overwhelmingly kind to others. There is enough variety in the way he spoke and acted to show him as a real person, someone being fully human, not just projecting a nice ministerial face. If we want others to discover God's love, we don't need to polish up our evangelism techniques; we need instead to be like Jesus. If we treat people with the same kind of honesty, grace, freedom and respect as he did, sooner or later others will want to search for the God we follow.

It has often struck me that this passage could be read as if Jesus had never met Simon, Andrew, James and John until the day he walked down the beach and called them to follow him. If that had been the case, it would have been an extraordinary thing for them simply to get up and leave without a second thought, and follow him wherever he went. Given the size of the community he came from, though, the more likely interpretation is that they had already known him for some time and had had some hunch that a call like this would come.

For us, answering God's call is not usually a matter of a

revelation that comes out of the blue and changes the course of our lives; rather, it is a growing awareness that something is changing underfoot. What we need to do, like these disciples, is to continue going about our work and everyday life, but to be poised and ready to get up and act when the moment comes. That's not to say we should live with our bags packed in the hall, but we can seek a balance by keeping at bay the kind of unnecessary clutter that weighs us down and limits our breathing space. If our lives are reasonably in order, then we can hear and respond when the call comes, whether it means a literal change of location or a more internal shift in direction.

This story shows two pairs of brothers leaving livelihoods, responsibilities and family ties in order to follow Jesus. There are plenty of over-the-top religious cults that take this kind of story literally, encouraging people to abandon their careers and families in order to commit themselves to their new community. But other parts of scripture teach us to take seriously our responsibilities to family, livelihood and property. Some of the New Testament documents lay out elaborate household codes (Ephesians 6:1–9; Colossians 3:18–22). It's thought that, in the first few decades after Christ's death, the expectation that he would physically return to earth within a few months or years led Christians to regard earthly responsibilities as temporary: once Christ returned, these things would no longer matter. A clear Christian ethic of responsibility for family and property began to emerge only a generation later. If this ethic shifted significantly even within the first few years of Christianity, how can the call of the first disciples illuminate our understanding of our own calling?

Firstly, I think the story highlights the all-consuming excitement that comes at moments of revelation. These disciples seem completely entranced by Jesus: at this moment, nothing else matters more than following him. There are times in our lives when it is good and right to be completely absorbed in new ideas, particularly such life-changing ideas as the person of Jesus Christ.

Secondly, the story suggests that it's only when we've discovered the capacity to leave everything to go for what's really important that we gain sufficient perspective to fit all the other parts of our life into their rightful place. To love our family or career is good and right, but to be limited by an overdeveloped sense of responsibility is not. Adults shouldn't be completely controlled by family or career concerns and, when this happens, perhaps some epiphany is needed to get them to 'put down their nets' and follow Jesus. God does not call us to abandon society or neglect the people we love, but he does call us to follow him first. Only then will we have the perspective to care for ourselves, love our families and serve our world.

Be happy

Jesus went throughout Galilee, teaching in their synagogues and proclaiming the good news of the kingdom and curing every disease and every sickness among the people. So his fame spread throughout all Syria, and they brought to him all the sick, those who were afflicted with various diseases and pains, demoniacs, epileptics, and paralytics, and he cured them. And great crowds followed him from Galilee, the Decapolis, Jerusalem, Judea, and from beyond the Jordan. When Jesus saw the crowds, he went up the mountain; and after he sat down, his disciples came to him. Then he began to speak, and taught them, saying: 'Blessed are the poor in spirit, for theirs is the kingdom of heaven. Blessed are those who mourn, for they will be comforted.'

MATTHEW 4:23—5:4

The fourth chapter of Matthew begins with Jesus encountering temptations in total solitude in the wilderness, working out his personal faith and priorities. It then moves through his choosing and drawing his friends and disciples around him, and it ends with a vast number of people following him. He makes a swift journey from privacy and solitude to celebrity and constant publicity.

It seems, though, that in his public ministry Jesus had a different set of priorities from most of his followers. Healing sickness wasn't an end in itself but it was the natural outworking of the kingdom he was preaching. Jesus' fame spread at least as much through the healings as through his teaching, and people came from far and wide to watch or receive the miracles. Yet Jesus regarded his mission as something much more than healing: his teaching was always focused on proclaiming the kingdom of God.

There's nothing wrong with bringing our needs to God. Here we see Jesus giving people the miracles they are asking for, and in some accounts he goes out of his way to seek out the sick in order to heal them. But he looked for followers who didn't want to know him just for the miracles he could do. We can't preach the gospel authentically and not get drawn into acts of compassion, but Jesus' miracles weren't an end in themselves; the kingdom of God isn't just a social programme. The gospel leads to radical personal commitment but it isn't a self-improvement course; it leads to public action but it isn't solely about political activism. Jesus wanted his disciples to grasp the whole picture.

The kingdom of God, says Jesus, belongs not to those who come along just to get their immediate physical or material needs met, but to those who know that they have great spiritual needs, for their deepest longing will be met in an encounter with God. This saying is the beginning of the Sermon on the Mount, which most scholars believe was never delivered as one whole speech but is Matthew's summary of quite a number of Jesus' teachings. The first few verses, known as the Beatitudes (5:3–12), are a list of things that make people 'happy' or 'blessed', but this is not the kind of happiness we get from, for instance, buying a new pair of shoes or going on a great date or a wonderful holiday. Instead, it's a sense of peace and confidence concerning what really matters.

We might have a bad day in the kingdom of God; we might

even have a bad year. But we can still know deep down that the situation is never utterly hopeless, never beyond rescue, never beyond the help and healing of God. Jesus didn't say, 'Follow me and you'll always be happy' but, 'Those people who know they have great spiritual needs are happy.' It sounds like a contradiction—but Jesus wasn't so much guaranteeing us happiness as redefining it. Happiness is not a trivial surface emotion that can be wiped out in an instant, but a profound state of peace and confidence that God is with us, come what may.

Questions for reflection

- Do we give enough freedom and encouragement for new experiments in church, knowing that some will fail and some will become the 'vintage' church of the future? What do we know about that might have the promise of being a future 'vintage'?
- 'In a society that is both over-indulgent and excessively body-conscious, perhaps one of the challenges of Lent is to befriend our own bodies...' In what ways do we need to take better care of our bodies? In what ways do we need to accept ourselves as we are?
- What kind of clutter is there in my life that makes me unprepared for following God? What one thing could I do to be more spiritually agile?

Other wildernesses

Misconceptions

[God said to Abraham], 'Take your son, your only son Isaac, whom you love, and go to the land of Moriah, and offer him there as a burnt-offering on one of the mountains that I shall show you.' So Abraham rose early in the morning, saddled his donkey, and took two of his young men with him, and his son Isaac; he cut the wood for the burnt-offering, and set out... On the third day Abraham looked up and saw the place far away. Then Abraham said to his young men, 'Stay here with the donkey; the boy and I will go over there; we will worship, and then we will come back to you.' Abraham took the wood of the burnt-offering and laid it on his son Isaac, and he himself carried the fire and the knife. So the two of them walked on together. Isaac said to his father Abraham, 'Father!' And he said, 'Here I am, my son.' He said, 'The fire and the wood are here, but where is the lamb for a burnt-offering?' Abraham said, 'God himself will provide the lamb for a burnt-offering, my son.' ...

When they came to the place that God had shown him, Abraham built an altar there and laid the wood in order. He bound his son Isaac, and laid him on the altar, on top of the wood. Then Abraham reached out his hand and took the knife to kill his son. But the angel of the Lord called to him from heaven, and said, 'Abraham, Abraham!' And he said, 'Here I am.' He said, 'Do not lay your hand on the boy or do anything to him; for now I know that you fear God, since you have not withheld your son, your only son, from me.' And Abraham looked up and saw a ram, caught in a thicket by its horns. Abraham went and took the ram and offered it up as a burnt-offering instead of his son. So Abraham called that place 'The Lord will provide'; as it is said to this day, 'On the mount of the Lord it shall be provided.'

The angel of the Lord called to Abraham a second time from heaven, and said, 'By myself I have sworn, says the Lord: Because you have done this, and have not withheld your son, your only son, I will indeed bless you, and I will make your offspring as numerous as the stars of heaven and as the sand that is on the seashore. And your offspring shall possess the gate of their enemies, and by your offspring shall all the nations of the earth gain blessing for themselves, because you have obeyed my voice.'

GENESIS 22:1–18 (ABRIDGED)

Recently my son and I read one of Roald Dahl's fantastic stories for children, *The BFG*. Everyone knows, don't they, that giants are terrible, bloodthirsty creatures? So when little Sophie was kidnapped by a giant in the middle of the night and carried far away to a land where giants live, naturally she was terrified. 'He is getting ready to eat me, she told herself. He will probably eat me raw, just as I am. Or perhaps he will boil me first.'[1] But as the story unfolds, Sophie discovers that her giant is in fact the Big *Friendly* Giant and the antithesis of all her fears. Gradually she begins to realise that all the things she expects to be horrifying are in fact benign. What she saw, and what she thought she saw, were not the same at all.

One of my favourite novels of the last decade is *Atonement* by Ian McEwan, which turns out to be another tale founded on a misconception. Thirteen-year-old Briony walks into a library and witnesses her sister locked in an act of passionate love, something so outside her youthful understanding that she mistakes it for an act of violence. This mistake later leads Briony to accuse her sister's boyfriend of a real act of violence. The rest of the book is Briony's act of atonement—writing and rewriting the story and its outcome as she dwells on the impact of her failure to understand and interpret and tell the truth. What she saw, and what she thought she saw, were not the same at all.

In the journey of faith we always start out with misconceptions and, in order to grow into God, we gradually have to unlearn ideas that may be deeply ingrained in us but are at odds with the truth. Our idea of God is drawn quite unconsciously from a mixture of sources: from experiences that go back to childhood, from media, from literature, from what we have heard or misheard in church and read or misread in the scriptures. These ideas are the baggage we bring with us to faith, so that God becomes, in our experience, a mixture of truth and misconception. The God we expect to meet may not be the same as the God we actually encounter.

In Genesis 22 we find Abraham toiling up a mountain in the belief that God is asking him to sacrifice his son—the son that God promised him in the first place, and on whom all his hopes of an heir depend. It's thought that child-sacrifice was common in Abraham's time and culture, so, despite a heavy heart, it would have seemed to him a reasonable thing for God to ask. Only when he arrives at the place of sacrifice does he realise that the appalling spectre of child-sacrifice is not within the kindness of his God.

Only four chapters earlier, Abraham had argued vehemently against God's proposed plan to destroy the city of Sodom, and in the end God changed his mind (Genesis 18:22–33). I wonder why Abraham didn't argue with God here in chapter 22? Perhaps, in fact, God wanted him to. Perhaps the point of the story was in part to raise the value of children. This story is often seen as prefiguring the eventual sacrifice of God's own Son as a sacrificial lamb, yet that in itself was far from Abraham's experience.

I wonder whether, perhaps, the whole point of God's 'test' of Abraham was precisely to teach Abraham that there are humane limits to what God will demand of people. We are just as prone as Abraham was to absorb cultural assumptions about religion and project them on to God, and we too seem easily persuaded that God expects us to make painful and even destructive sacrifices for the sake of religious principles. It's not uncommon for people to stay too long in abusive and destructive relationships because they believe they are required by God to be faithful come what may; or to devote years to deadening church situations because they believe they are called to stay; or to pursue ideas of vocation with a stoicism that is born not of love but of fear. Like Abraham on Mount Moriah, we need to identify the humane limits to what God demands of us, and to see that sometimes the sacrifices we make are born of our misconceptions, not of God's call. Although the trip up the mountain in Genesis 22 is described as a test of faith, I think it's less a test of how much gritty determination we have than a test of our attentiveness to the discovery of what God is really like.

It seems that we are very slow to believe in grace. Even in the church, where grace should be understood, it's common to find an emphasis on a 'righteousness' that has more to do with living up to people's expectations than with emulating God. What is it that underlies our preference for judgment over mercy, when everywhere the Bible calls us to understand God as being quick to forgive and restore? It's not as if God is soft on justice, but his move to grace is always swifter and more outrageously generous than we allow for.

Wilfred Owen saw that it is pride that interferes with our ability to live in grace. His 1918 poem 'The parable of the old man and the young' uses the story of Genesis 22 and begins with lines that closely emulate the King James Bible: 'So Abram rose, and clave the wood, and went, and took the fire with him, and a knife...'. He then blends the story of Abraham's altar with imagery of World War I: 'Then Abram bound the youth with belts and straps and builded parapets and trenches there...' Owen takes the angel's words, 'Lay not thy hand upon the lad', as a call to stop the senselessness of a protracted and bloody war. The ram caught in the thicket, which could be offered instead of the boy, is pride: 'Behold! Caught in a thicket by its horns, A Ram. Offer the Ram of Pride instead.' But departing from the Genesis story, Owen's poem ends with one of the most heartbreaking couplets in the English literature:

But the old man would not so, but slew his son,
And half the seed of Europe, one by one.[2]

The poem encapsulates perfectly the way in which God calls us to grace and gentleness and reconciliation, and we fail to listen, fail to hear, fail to understand. Owen is doubtless right that pride leads us to act harshly in the name of justice, when really what's called for is grace; perhaps we are also inhibited by fear that if we give an inch in our spiritual standards, everything we believe in will fall away from us. Whether through pride or fear or for other reasons, the picture of God that's deeply entrenched in our souls may be as skewed as Abraham's was.

Allowing our idea of God to change and grow is no easy task. My own experience is that there are times when I have held on for dear life to ideas I believed were central to faith, only to grow slowly into the realisation that I was mistaken.

While I was taking my first degree in theology, most of the building blocks of my faith came up for serious re-examination. I remember asking one of my professors how it was possible for faith to survive this kind of intense intellectual scrutiny. He thought for a while and then said, 'Once upon a time I believed in a great many things. Now I believe only in a few things, but I believe in them more deeply than I ever thought possible. That God is, that God is love, that Jesus is the Son of God—these things I believe. Everything else is up for debate.' I never forgot his words and I began to allow my own rather stern vision of God to mellow. Gradually the God who, it seemed, always demanded more than I was able to give began to give way to a God who breathed love and kindness and freedom into my heart.

Unanswered questions

One day the heavenly beings came to present themselves before the Lord, and Satan also came among them to present himself before the Lord. The Lord said to Satan, 'Where have you come from?' Satan answered the Lord, 'From going to and fro on the earth, and from walking up and down on it.' The Lord said to Satan, 'Have you considered my servant Job? There is no one like him on the earth, a blameless and upright man who fears God and turns away from evil. He still persists in his integrity, although you incited me against him, to destroy him for no reason.' Then Satan answered the Lord, 'Skin for skin! All that people have they will give to save their lives. But stretch out your hand now and touch his bone and his flesh, and he will curse you to your face.' The Lord said to Satan, 'Very well, he is in your power; only spare his life.'

So Satan went out from the presence of the Lord, and inflicted loathsome sores on Job from the sole of his foot to the crown of his head. Job took a potsherd with which to scrape himself, and sat among the ashes.

Then his wife said to him, 'Do you still persist in your integrity? Curse God, and die.' But he said to her, 'You speak as any foolish woman would speak. Shall we receive the good at the hand of God, and not receive the bad?' In all this Job did not sin with his lips.

Now when Job's three friends heard of all these troubles that had come upon him, each of them set out from his home—Eliphaz the Temanite, Bildad the Shuhite, and Zophar the Naamathite. They met together to go and console and comfort him. When they saw him from a distance, they did not recognise him, and they raised their voices and wept aloud; they tore their robes and threw dust in the air upon their heads. They sat with him on the ground for seven days and seven nights, and no one spoke a word to him, for they saw that his suffering was very great.

JOB 2

The second of our wilderness characters is Job, who, in the midst of intense suffering, goes out and sits on a heap of ashes, symbolising his own death. Like many ancient stories, it's hard to be sure how much of it is historical and how much has been stylised to make a point. In a sense, though, it doesn't matter, because either way the point is to tell us something about the human condition. Job's story is told as a dark comedy—a tale of misadventure in which everything comes right in the end—and, like the characters in a Shakespeare play, Job and his wife and friends are true to life, and bring home some of the most pertinent and timeless religious questions.

The main point of Job's story is to challenge the idea that suffering is brought upon us for a reason. Job is not alone in his grief: he still has his wife and three friends, and one by one they tell him why they believe he is suffering and what he should do about it. Michael Buckley, an American Jesuit, once said that the main cause of atheism is bad theism: it's a catchy statement that doesn't bear too close an analysis, but the germ of truth within it is that bad theology can lead people to reject God on the basis of spurious ideas. Job's wife and friends articulate a series of half-truths and popular but flawed ideas about God and human suffering.

Job's wife points out, with no small degree of wifely irritation, that he has always lived a life of integrity and always honoured God. If God doesn't reward him with blessings and good things, she asks, what's the point? She sees no point in continuing to worship God and utters the famous words, 'Curse God and die' (v. 9), for which she is often given short shrift by preachers.

Looking at it from a purely human point of view, Job's wife has my sympathy. Within the space of a few hours, she too has been plunged from riches to poverty and has been informed of the death of all their sheep and cattle, all their servants and all her children. Then, in the midst of her desolation, her husband contracts a painful and disfiguring disease. Her response echoes a familiar theme in the face of deep suffering. We've seen some terrible natural disasters in the past decade and one response at such times is the question hurled at God, or at those who believe in him, 'How can you worship a God who sits by and lets this kind of suffering continue?'

The error that Job's wife articulates is the assumption that the point of religion is to get blessings. Put crudely, it's a kind of slot-machine theology: if you obey God, God will reward you. If God doesn't reward you, what's the point in religion? 'Curse God and die' is a response to a God who has not lived up to the expectations of this kind of deal. But Job wanted something more than a material exchange with God. He wanted God to answer him.

Job's friends also pronounce some of the worst theology in the world (which subsequently gets challenged and over-turned), but I have to say that on one level I wouldn't mind having friends like these. Many of us find other people's grief so difficult to face that, for fear of saying the wrong thing, we keep a polite distance. Job's friends understood that a grieving person still needs their friends to be there, even if they can't think of anything to say. What they say, several times over in different ways, is that Job must be responsible for his suffering, based on the assumption that what we get from God (or the gods) is always in proportion to what we deserve. 'What did I do to deserve this?' is a question that links suffering to our own actions, either because we think we did something that deserved punishment or because we feel unfairly treated.

Was there any truth in what Job's wife and friends had to say? After all, Job's continued insistence that he had not sinned goes against most religious sensibilities. Paul wrote that 'all have sinned and fall short of the glory of God' (Romans 3:23)—but to apply isolated quotes like that can turn truth into truism. Job, I think, rather than claiming he was perfect, was asking a deeper question and insisting, rightly, that if his suffering were a punishment, then it was wildly out of proportion to what he deserved. This gets closer to the genuine crisis in suffering when a young mother gets cancer, or when children are harmed through natural disaster or through the carelessness or wickedness of others. The issue in those circumstances is nothing to do with whether or not 'all have sinned…'; it's about the conviction that nobody deserves such punishment.

Job's part in the story was to challenge the prevailing opinions. He certainly didn't say that suffering doesn't matter. In fact, he railed against God, pleaded with God to help him and demanded an answer to his questions, and in doing so he voiced one of our deepest questions: why does God let bad things happen to good people?

On one level, Job's story calls us to give up the idea that religion is a kind of 'deal' with God. Prayer doesn't work like a slot machine; there's no formula whereby, if we do or say the right things, we get the answer we want. Prayer is an engagement with God, sometimes involving a brutal wrestling match until we see him more clearly. If we walk away too soon, if we discount God because he doesn't behave as we think he should or give us the answers we need, then we underestimate what the Christian journey is all about.

On another level, though, what Job discovers is that even the answers to his questions are not really what he was looking for. Perhaps part of his frustration with his friends was not so much that he disagreed with their theology but that he knew that reasoning out his suffering was never going to help. Even the right theology wouldn't make it better. If you read to the end of the story, you'll find that when God does appear to Job, he doesn't explain why the innocent suffer or give a reason why our prayers are sometimes answered and other times not. Instead, God's answer to Job is to meet him in the midst of the suffering. The result is that Job's story neither domesticates God nor leaves him beyond comprehension. Instead, the God of all creation touches Job at the most intimate place of human need, and Job discovers that what he wanted all along was not explanation but encounter, not rationality but relationship.

The truth of the matter is that when theology is divorced from engagement, it becomes hollow, and, however fascinating theology is to study, when we're faced with the stark realities of life no theory will help us. The power of Job's story is not that it replaces flawed theology with good theology but that it shows that our questions are resolved, ultimately, in being met by God.

Turn aside and see

Moses was keeping the flock of his father-in-law Jethro, the priest of Midian; he led his flock beyond the wilderness, and came to Horeb, the mountain of God. There the angel of the Lord appeared to him in a flame of fire out of a bush; he looked, and the bush was blazing, yet it was not consumed. Then Moses said, 'I must turn aside and look at this great sight, and see why the bush is not burned up.' When the Lord saw that he had turned aside to see, God called to him out of the bush, 'Moses, Moses!' And he said, 'Here I am.'

EXODUS 3:1–4

Moses was born to a family of Hebrew slaves but brought up in an Egyptian palace. In adulthood, he murdered an Egyptian and had to flee for his life. He went into hiding in the desert, where he married the daughter of a nomadic shepherd who was also a Midianite priest. By the time he saw the burning bush, Moses was middle-aged, still living in the desert and still looking after his father-in-law's sheep. I think we could reasonably say that Moses had got into a rut. He'd made a couple of major mistakes early on, and now he was still lurking below the parapet for fear of being found out. As a result, he wasn't sure any more who he was or what his purpose was in life. He was just settled in for the long haul somewhere comfortable that paid the bills, but it wasn't what he'd dreamed of when he was young and it wasn't his heart's desire.

On this particular day, Moses led the sheep out to new pasture in the foothills of Mount Horeb. He had no idea, of course, that he was about to meet God. When he saw the bush, he didn't know why it seemed to be on fire and yet not burning up. All he knew was that he had spotted something bright and sparkly, something intriguing and very exciting. 'I must turn aside,' he said, 'and see...'. Moses dared to step out of his routine, left the sheep to look after themselves and followed where his intellectual curiosity led him. It was only then that he heard God's voice calling his name.

Often, when we think about the idea of God's call, we end up trying too hard to figure out what it is that God is saying to us. We tend to think that our calling must be something obviously Christian, the kind of thing we call a 'ministry'. Sometimes we thrash around trying to fit ourselves into some existing ministry or project, or trying to meet some unfilled needs, and yet we end up feeling like Moses—settled in for the long haul but wondering whether we've missed our dreams. In addition, especially if it's good work that we're involved in, we may feel guilty for not being sufficiently enthused about what we're doing.

If you think you hear a call that gives you a sense of gloom and despondency, a loss of energy and interest, a feeling of joyless obligation, than it may be God's call to somebody else but it is almost certainly not his call to you. Jesus didn't say, 'You have to give up being yourself to have a ministry'; he said, 'The kingdom of God is within you' (Luke 17:21, NIV). Jesus didn't say, 'My call is heavy and difficult'; he said, 'My yoke is easy and my burden is light' (Matthew 11:30). When Moses dared to break out of his routine and went to look at something that fascinated him, he discovered that his natural curiosity did not lead him away from God at all; rather, it led him into an encounter with God that transformed his life. It was precisely through Moses' act of following what he thought interesting that God eventually turned him from an isolated shepherd into a political reformer and religious leader.

If we try to fit into a mould that wasn't made for us, we become stiff and inflexible. We mustn't let the fear of losing our faith limit our imagination and our sense of adventure. When we allow our natural gifts and inclinations to lead us— whether into the world of history or medicine, computers or astrophysics, music, art or literature—that's when we see clearly who we are and what we're meant to do with the gifts we've been given. That's where we hear God calling to us, and that's where God is able to speak through us to others.

Eric Liddell was a Scotsman, a missionary, a rugby player and a runner—so fast that he was nicknamed the Flying Scotsman. Eric and his brothers and sister were born in China and were committed to the idea of returning there as missionaries after they'd completed their education in Britain. But when Liddell's amazing talent for running was spotted, he was recruited for the 1924 British Olympic team. Liddell's story was immortalised in the 1981 film *Chariots of Fire*, which showed how he faced up to various conflicts between his faith and his natural gifts. In the film, the conflict is crystallised in a conversation that Liddell has with his sister. They walk up into the hills overlooking Edinburgh, to a rocky outcrop known as Arthur's Seat, and there his sister urges him to give up all this nonsense with running and rugby, and concentrate on what's really important—the calling of the Lord to missionary work. Eric replies that he knows very well that God has called them back to China. 'I believe God made me for a purpose,' he says. 'But he also made me *fast*! And when I run, I feel his pleasure.'

Eric Liddell won a gold medal for Britain in 1924; in 1925 he returned to China as a missionary and stayed there until his death 20 years later. His mission work was dedicated and valuable, and he made use of his athletic skills in building every community he worked in, as well as teaching the English language and the Bible. Yet his most enduring sermon to the world, his most resounding statement about faith, came not through his 'Christian' work but through his commitment to doing what he did best of all—running.

Put aside what other people say you ought to do, and put aside your own mental commentary about what you think God will make you do. Instead, do what Moses did. Follow whatever you find intriguing, intellectually or artistically stimulating; go where your curiosity and your natural gifts lead you; and when you do, keep an ear open, because sooner or later you will hear the voice of God whispering your name.

Do not come near

God called to him out of the bush, 'Moses, Moses!' And he said, 'Here am I.' Then he said, 'Do not come near; put off your shoes from your feet, for the place on which you are standing is holy ground.' And he said, 'I am the God of your father, the God of Abraham, the God of Isaac, and the God of Jacob.' And Moses hid his face, for he was afraid to look at God.

Then the Lord said, 'I have seen the affliction of my people who are in Egypt, and have heard their cry because of their taskmasters; I know their sufferings, and I have come down to deliver them out of the hand of the Egyptians, and to bring them up out of that land to a good and broad land, a land flowing with milk and honey, to the place of the Canaanites, the Hittites, the Amorites, the Perizzites, the Hivites, and the Jebusites. And now, behold, the cry of the people of Israel has come to me, and I have seen the oppression with which the Egyptians oppress them. Come, I will send you to Pharaoh that you may bring forth my people, the sons of Israel, out of Egypt.' But Moses said to God, 'Who am I that I should go to Pharaoh, and bring the sons of Israel out of Egypt?' He said, 'But I will be with you; and this shall be the sign for you, that I have sent you: when you have brought forth the people out of Egypt, you shall serve God upon this mountain.'

Then Moses said to God, 'If I come to the people of Israel and say to them, "The God of your fathers has sent me to you," and they ask me, "What is his name?" what shall I say to them?' God said to Moses, 'I am who I am.' And he said, 'Say this to the people of Israel, "I am has sent me to you."'

EXODUS 3:4–14 (RSV)

Everyone agrees that junk mail is annoying but one of its most irritating features is the way that, through the use of a database, something entirely impersonal fakes a personal touch by having your name and address on it. By contrast, one of life's pleasures is the warmth and interest you feel when a real letter—especially if it's handwritten—falls through the letterbox. We know when we're being addressed genuinely and personally, and so it's no wonder that when Moses heard his name called from the burning bush, his response was immediate. God wasn't calling out to just any old passer-by who happened to be listening. He was calling Moses, and him specifically, to a task for which he was supremely suited.

This call, though, was intimidating as well as intimate; it repelled at the same time as it attracted. God called Moses by name but, when Moses replied, God said, 'Do not come near' and told him to take off his shoes. Come near, God seemed to be saying, but not too near. A personal call doesn't imply a casual intimacy or eliminate the transcendence and mystery of God. Moses found himself stripped bare, known in person, called in love and yet filled with awe and at a loss for words.

From this we can learn something about what we should expect when we worship and pray. If we think of God with too much distance, we fail to grasp that we are called by name. God is not just the God of the world, the God of the Church, or the God of the minister or priest, but *my* God—a God who knows me by name and calls me to serve him. At the same time, focusing too closely on this personal knowledge can fool us into thinking that we have more intimacy with God than we really do; it can make God too small, too much like a supersized human being, a superhuman father or brother figure who is at our beck and call.

If we fail to grasp the mystery and transcendence of God, our approach to worship will certainly lack humility but, worse than that, it will disable us from seeing and hearing the truth of God. It seems to me that one of the greatest dangers of organised religion is its power to persuade us that we understand God and have some easy purchase on him, giving us an exaggerated sense of his favour. Without detracting from the fact that love is the very essence of God, we need to take infinite care not to domesticate God, not to clothe our idea of God with our own preferences and our own wishes. As soon as we cease to be surprised and disturbed by the infinite, we have made our expectations too small, and once again we will need to be both called by name and held back by transcendence.

On Monday we read that when God finally answered Job, the answers were not the ones he thought he was looking for. Yesterday we saw that Moses discovered a real encounter with God only by stepping outside what he already knew. In both cases, their actual encounter with God was surprisingly unlike what they had anticipated. The lesson seems to be that whenever we think we know what to expect of God, the reality is bound to be something different. A true encounter will always surprise us, either by being more deeply personal than we thought possible or by shaking our assumptions that we understand God at all and returning us, barefoot and bewildered, to holy ground.

To accept that God will always surprise us is not the same as the heresy of modalism—the idea that God hides behind a mask, concealing a face of wrathful judgment behind a cover of loving-kindness. God's essence is always congruent with his attributes. It's more the idea that God is perceived by us only when we recognise that God is not just a super-sized me, that we have to launch into the invisible in order to see him. We walk by faith, not by sight (2 Corinthians 5:7).

Giving up our preconceived ideas about God in order to discover the true God is an idea that was explored at length by the early Desert Father, John Cassian, who said that in order to meet God in truth, three kinds of renunciation are necessary. Firstly, Cassian said, we have 'to give up our attachment to possessions, although this in itself will not bring us into communion with God. Secondly, we have to give up our unshakeable habits and vices. In other words, giving up things for their own sake is mere stoicism and of no particular value; it's detaching ourselves from our dependence upon them that counts.

The third renunciation that Cassian describes is about leaving behind our inherited perceptions of God in order to see him clearly. He illustrates his idea with the story of Abraham being called to leave his native land and his father's house, seeing this as a metaphor for leaving behind the picture of God that we have picked up from all sorts of sources. Most people, whether they accept or reject God, have a picture of God that is made up of bits and pieces of teaching or reading, together with images of authority that they have encountered. Cassian's point is that wherever we have picked up our idea of God, it is imperfect, and only by consciously relinquishing those impressions will we free our minds to encounter the invisible reality of God.[3]

Antoine de Saint Exupéry wrote in *Le Petit Prince*, '*Voici mon secret. Il est très simple: on ne voit bien qu'avec le coeur. L'essentiel est invisible pour les yeux.*' ('Here is my secret. It is simple: you can only see well with the heart. What's essential is invisible to the eye.')[4] We get a clear glimpse of God only when we are willing to let go our preformed ideas of what God is like and allow a new picture to form—one that goes beyond our senses. The true God, the God who calls us by name and then tells us not to come near, is a God who startles us out of our comfort zone, exceeds our greatest hopes, asks more than we believe we are capable of and gives us more than we think we deserve. This is a God who, in the words of the writer to the Ephesians, is 'able to accomplish abundantly far more than all we can ask or imagine' (3:20). So while we do well to search for God and to try the best we can to understand him, we should never fool ourselves that we have come into a comfortably close relationship to him. If we domesticate God, we will find that he has somehow slipped out of the back door. We can no more penetrate the layers of mystery than we can see beyond the horizon.

Peering through the fog

The Lord said to Moses, 'Come up to me on the mountain, and wait there; and I will give you the tablets of stone, with the law and the commandment, which I have written for their instruction.' So Moses set out with his assistant Joshua, and Moses went up into the mountain of God. To the elders he had said, 'Wait here for us, until we come to you again; for Aaron and Hur are with you; whoever has a dispute may go to them.' Then Moses went up on the mountain, and the cloud covered the mountain. The glory of the Lord settled on Mount Sinai, and the cloud covered it for six days; on the seventh day he called to Moses out of the cloud. Now the appearance of the glory of the Lord was like a devouring fire on the top of the mountain in the sight of the people of Israel. Moses entered the cloud, and went up on the mountain. Moses was on the mountain for forty days and forty nights.

EXODUS 24:12–18

I live in East Anglia, close to the Fens, an area that is mostly good for visibility. As the locals say in defence of the mountainless landscape that gives rise to the best skyscapes in England, 'There's nothing to spoil the view!' In the winter, though, under certain conditions you can find yourself moving in a matter of minutes from clear crisp air to a dense fog that hangs just a few feet above the flat, damp fields—the kind of fog that forces you, if you're driving, to drop your speed to a crawl because you can see barely 20 feet ahead.

Over the last couple of days, we've read about Moses' first encounter with God, and how he was attracted to the strange sight of a bush that was alight and yet not burning. He was entranced by what he saw and, although he was not searching for God, as he looked into the bright clear flame, he unmistakably heard God's voice. Now, some time later, Moses sets out deliberately to hear God's voice, but, far from seeing something bright and clear, he finds himself surrounded by a dense cloud. How is it that when he wasn't particularly seeking God, he saw with clarity and brilliance, but years later he could perceive God only through the cover of clouds?

One way of making sense of this puzzle was offered by Gregory of Nyssa. Gregory, his brother Basil the Great, and Gregory Nazianzen were Christian leaders in the fourth century, known as the Cappadocian Fathers. Late in life, Gregory of Nyssa wrote a meditation called *Life of Moses*, which isn't a biographical account but uses each episode in Moses' story as an illustration of the spiritual life. So, for instance, the deliverance from slavery in Egypt is taken as a representation of deliverance from darkness and sin, and the promised land represents heaven. Gregory viewed Moses' progression from the light to the cloud as an allegory of the spiritual journey. His vision of God in the light of the burning bush signifies the soul's epiphany of God: God is seen in the light. But having once seen and encountered God, the soul needs to grasp something of God's hidden nature, which is symbolized by the cloud.

One of the things I like about Gregory's reasoning is the way he makes sense of one of the conundrums of the spiritual life. You might expect that the longer you live as a Christian, and the closer you walk to God, the clearer your vision of God would become. Yet, contrary to expectations, the reality seems to be the other way round. The longer we know God, the more there is to know, and the more we see that God is, in some sense, quite unknowable. As C.S. Lewis put it, Aslan is 'not a tame lion'.[5]

Perhaps the movement from the light to the cloud is a bit like Paul's idea of progressing from milk to meat (1 Corinthians 3:1–2). Infants can digest only milk, but adults can and should eat food that is harder work: we have to cut up meat, choose what is edible and leave the bones, then chew it and take time to digest it. Food for adults is hard work but it's much more interesting! Similarly, our initial encounter with God needs to have some clarity about it or we'd never get started, but if the continuing journey was always transparently easy, it would rapidly become dull and boring—not only because of the lack of challenge to us but because it is quite impossible to know anything of God in depth without stepping outside what comes easily. The clarity of light only gives us a surface knowledge of God. If we are to know something of a God who is, in essence, quite other than us, then at some point we have to struggle through the fog of incomprehension to gain deeper understanding.

When I was an undergraduate, one of the posters that hung on my wall was a photograph of a large, self-satisfied gorilla, with the caption, 'The more you study, the more you know. The more you know, the more you forget. The more you forget, the less you know. So why study?' There's something of the same dynamic here. It's an appealing idea that we could go on for ever seeing God clearly in the light but, as soon as we begin to know anything about God, we find that he is constantly moving.

We have to keep moving, too, even though it means finding our way through the clouds, if our spiritual experience is to be real and not a fantasy. Driving through a fenland fog isn't fun, and to get to your destination safely takes patience and care, but moving slowly and carefully, paying close attention, you find that although the skyline has disappeared you can perceive enough of the road underneath to get home. Repeating the experience over time, you gradually learn the shape of the roads so that you don't depend only on clarity of vision but on a deep understanding of the route. We need not fear disappearing into the clouds in search of God: we'll discover that even though the landscape of God is only ever partly visible, we'll find our way home all the same.

You shall see my back

Moses said to the Lord, 'See, you have said to me, "Bring up this people"; but you have not let me know whom you will send with me. Yet you have said, "I know you by name, and you have also found favour in my sight." Now if I have found favour in your sight, show me your ways, so that I may know you and find favour in your sight. Consider too that this nation is your people.' He said, 'My presence will go with you, and I will give you rest.' And he said to him, 'If your presence will not go, do not carry us up from here. For how shall it be known that I have found favour in your sight, I and your people, unless you go with us? In this way, we shall be distinct, I and your people, from every people on the face of the earth.'

The Lord said to Moses, 'I will do the very thing that you have asked; for you have found favour in my sight, and I know you by name.' Moses said, 'Show me your glory, I pray.' And he said, 'I will make all my goodness pass before you, and will proclaim before you the name, "The Lord"; and I will be gracious to whom I will be gracious, and will show mercy on whom I will show mercy. But', he said, 'you cannot see my face; for no one shall see me and live.' And the Lord continued, 'See, there is a place by me where you shall stand on the rock; and while my glory passes by I will put you in a cleft of the rock, and I will cover you with my hand until I have passed by; then I will take away my hand, and you shall see my back; but my face shall not be seen.'

EXODUS 33:12–23

God, we are told, spoke to Moses as a person speaks to a friend, yet the closer Moses gets to God, the more he feels he doesn't really know him. His yearning to see God face to face is a longing to penetrate beyond the mystery and know God as he really is.

To say that we long to see God clearly, or to see Jesus face to face, may be a genuine statement of devotion, yet (since we are told that no one can see God face to face and live) by implication it means that we are ready to give up this life— something that, in reality, most of us are not ready to do. In the biblical accounts, whenever someone gets a glimpse of the glory of God, they are powerfully affected by it—falling down in a faint, for instance, or being rendered absolutely speechless (Revelation 1:17; Luke 1:22). The idea here is that, faced with the full revelation of God, a mortal being would be incapable of surviving the impact. By declining Moses' request, God is saying in effect that Moses' life is not over yet. It's part of the constraint of human life that we cannot see beyond the horizon of eternity.

Why, though, if Moses is not allowed to see God as he is, would God show Moses his departing back? What does this reveal that is more than the cloud and yet less than the full-on revelation of God's essence?

Yesterday we considered Gregory of Nyssa's idea of the progression from seeing God clearly in the light to seeing God's hidden nature through the cloud. This third major encounter, where Moses sees only God's retreating back, is taken by

Gregory to be a further progression into the knowledge of God. This time, Gregory says, 'as the soul makes progress, [and] by greater and more perfect concentration, comes to appreciate what the knowledge of truth is... so much the more does it see that the divine nature is invisible.'[6] In other words, the clarity of understanding that seems to come through the senses barely scratches the surface; the truer vision of God emerges only when the soul is guided through sense perception to the invisible world.

Gregory's approach to theology is conditioned by the fact that God is ultimately wrapped in mystery and, in the end, cannot be defined. This way of talking about God is known as apophatic or negative theology, not in the sense that it has negative overtones but because whenever we try to say what God is like, the best we can manage is a crude approximation. We are able to say with absolute clarity only what God is not: God is not evil, not ignorant, not divided. Apophatic theology, then, is motivated by the recognition that although God has revealed himself to us in various ways, and most clearly through incarnation, there is still a sense in which we cannot pin him down. Moses yearns to see God as he is; God says that he may see his glory (or his 'beauty', as Gregory puts it) but not his face. He can see enough of God to know what is knowable but the ultimate vision, looking right into the core of God's nature, is simply not possible for Moses or for any human being to endure.

Gregory understood this to demonstrate a further stage of progress towards knowing God. Having first encountered God in the clarity of light, and later in mystery, the journey into God gradually brings us to admit that God is never finally knowable to us—not in this life, at any rate.

What Gregory is driving at is that it's naïve to imagine we can see God clearly. It's only when we begin to perceive God as he is that we realise that we can't really see him at all. It seems a little unfair, perhaps, to suggest that the deeper we move into the knowledge of God, the less able we are to see him, but invisibility is not the same thing as absence; invisibility doesn't wipe out the sense that God is present. Although God himself cannot be seen, we can see where he has been. God is beyond us, different and other, not knowable in our terms and through our senses, yet the attributes of God can be clearly seen and understood and articulated. It's interesting, then, that when God makes himself present, though invisible, to Moses, he announces himself in terms of his attributes: 'merciful and gracious, slow to anger, and abounding in steadfast love and faithfulness, keeping steadfast love for the thousandth generation, forgiving iniquity...' (Exodus 34:6–7). God's essence may be for ever beyond the horizon but the effects of his presence are knowable.

The rabbinic tradition suggests that to see God's back means 'where he has just been'. In other words, we are incapable of observing or experiencing the presence of God directly or in the moment that it occurs, but we can see it retrospectively: we can realise that God's presence was here just a moment ago. That seeming miracle of human kindness, that act of unbounded generosity, that impulse for self-giving, that moment of stillness and beauty, that reverie of tranquillity—it's only when the moment has passed that we register something of the holy. Rarely, rarely do we stand, like Moses in hushed places, feeling the impulse to kneel or to remove our shoes. Mostly we see the traces of God's glory in the shadow of his presence as he passes by.

Loss of nerve

When the people saw that Moses delayed to come down from the mountain, the people gathered around Aaron and said to him, 'Come, make gods for us, who shall go before us; as for this Moses, the man who brought us up out of the land of Egypt, we do not know what has become of him.' Aaron said to them, 'Take off the gold rings that are on the ears of your wives, your sons, and your daughters, and bring them to me.' So all the people took off the gold rings from their ears, and brought them to Aaron. He took the gold from them, formed it in a mould, and cast an image of a calf; and they said, 'These are your gods, O Israel, who brought you up out of the land of Egypt!' When Aaron saw this, he built an altar before it; and Aaron made proclamation and said, 'Tomorrow shall be a festival to the Lord.' They rose early the next day, and offered burnt-offerings and brought sacrifices of well-being; and the people sat down to eat and drink, and rose up to revel.

The Lord said to Moses, 'Go down at once! Your people, whom you brought up out of the land of Egypt, have acted perversely; they have been quick to turn aside from the way that I commanded them; they have cast for themselves an image of a calf, and have worshipped it and sacrificed to it... I have seen this people, how stiff-necked they are. Now let me alone, so that my wrath may burn hot against them and I may consume them; and of you I will make a great nation.'

But Moses implored the Lord his God, and said, 'O Lord, why does your wrath burn hot against your people, whom you brought out of the land of Egypt with great power and with a mighty hand? Why should the Egyptians say, "It was with evil intent that he brought them out to kill them in the mountains, and to consume them from the face of the earth"? Turn from your fierce wrath; change your mind and do not bring disaster on your people. Remember Abraham, Isaac, and Israel, your servants, how you swore to them by your own self, saying to them, "I will multiply your descendants like the stars of heaven, and all this land that I have promised I will give to your descendants, and they shall inherit it for ever."' And the Lord changed his mind about the disaster that he planned to bring on his people.

EXODUS 32:1–14 (ABRIDGED)

Over the last few days we've looked at Moses' own spiritual journey through the wilderness, but his journey was not taken in isolation. In fact, the whole point of his calling was to lead his people out of Egypt, through the wilderness and into the land of promise. We noted at the beginning of this journey through Lent that the traditional fast was not individually chosen but a community event, with each person taking part in the same fast. So before we leave these meditations on the wilderness, let's look at what was happening to the people of Israel as a community and what happened to their perception of God as they followed Moses through the desert.

In the biblical accounts, mountains almost always symbolise epiphany, for it's often on mountaintops that God gives people a clear revelation of himself. Here we find Moses advancing up the mountain to receive, on behalf of the whole community, God's new revelation. Back down in the foothills, however, the people, tired and dull from their journey through the wilderness, begin to lose sight of where they are going, and look back to where they have come from. Their old life in Egypt had been unbearable to them while they were there; it was a life of slavery that they were only too glad to leave behind. Yet it seems that they had not banked on such a lengthy and difficult journey towards the promise. We live in an 'instant' culture, a society that has lived for decades on the idea of credit, buying now and paying later, with debt and economic instability as one of the resulting problems. It's a mindset that's easy to fall into, and it can affect more than just our attitude to material things. In spiritual terms, too, we give up easily and think we can take the waiting out of wanting.

If we subconsciously absorb the idea that faith is just another consumer durable, when it doesn't deliver us health and happiness the temptation is to blame church structures, denominations, ministers, worship leaders, or whoever it is that seems to be failing to deliver. True faith, though, has always been a matter of spiritual discipline: we can't reach the land of promise without trudging through the wilderness, which demands personal, individual effort. It also demands that we walk together as a community, in the company of those we find annoying and slow as well as those we like and admire.

The Israelites looked back to the place where they had previously been enslaved, and suddenly it didn't seem so bad. Dry-mouthed in the desert, they forgot the hopelessness of captivity and remembered only that there had been melons to eat. Instead of enduring hardship and uncertainty for the sake of the promise of a bigger, freer space, they reverted to the rituals of faith associated with their enslavement: they melted down their earrings and coins and made a golden calf, one of the gods of ancient Egypt.

As we have seen, one of the certainties of growing spiritually is that we have to leave behind lesser visions of God in order for the truth to come into focus. It takes vision and energy to leave behind imperfect ideas that keep our lives small and contained, enslaved in routines that are ultimately deadening, but shedding old ways of thinking doesn't lead to an instant metamorphosis. Adventuring into the unknown is a process, following something that may be as intangible and temporary as a pillar of light or cloud, until eventually something new materialises beneath our feet.

Setting out on a spiritual adventure is easy, but it's much harder to persist until it becomes real and sure. In the process, it takes immense courage and patience to resist the temptation either to go back to an old formula or to give up altogether. When a new vision doesn't seem to be working out, the answer is not to sentimentalise the place we've come from. Instead, we need to hold our nerve and wait until the new revelation emerges.

The function of community in this story is worth noticing. There's a great deal of discussion about how leadership should function in the church today and, partly in response to some heavy-handed models of hierarchy, there are those who field the idea that a community doesn't need a leader. The truth is that leaders are always present and, if a community doesn't choose its leaders, they will soon emerge by default or self-appointment. In the absence of Moses and Joshua, the Israelites turned to Aaron, another leading figure in the community. If only Aaron had said 'no' to their ideas, perhaps the story would have turned out differently, but Aaron (a somewhat unwilling leader) let the majority take charge. The word of the people was loud and clear and it was carried without debate. It's hard to be the person who speaks out against the majority view but popular opinion isn't always right and, if anyone could have stopped the proceedings and called for a debate, it was Aaron.

Who knows what might have happened if he had taken up that responsibility?

It's interesting that the location for this communal loss of nerve was right in the foothills of the mountain. They were so close to the revelation—so near the place where God was about to appear. Sometimes I think we can endure long desert experiences, yet it's just as things are about to change—just as we are, metaphorically speaking, at the foot of the mountain of revelation—that we lose confidence and look back. It's worth remembering not only that our actions and words may affect the spiritual progress of those around us, but also that when we lose confidence in the journey we've embarked upon, we may in fact be within striking distance of a new glimpse of God.

Questions for reflection

- In what way do we consider ourselves to have a close and intimate relationship to God? How are those ideas balanced with an understanding of mystery and transcendence?
- What are the images of God with which we began our spiritual journey, or that we hold most dear? Are we willing to allow those ideas to be held up to scrutiny?
- What spiritual journeys have we grown tired of? What adventures now seem unbelievable to us? Are we in a cul-de-sac or in the foothills of the mountain?

Changing perceptions

Lost and found (1):
the lost coin

'What woman, having ten silver coins, if she loses one coin, does not light a lamp and sweep the house and seek diligently until she finds it? And when she has found it, she calls together her friends and neighbours, saying, "Rejoice with me, for I have found the coin that I had lost." Just so, I tell you, there is joy before the angels of God over one sinner who repents.'

LUKE 15:8–10 (ESV)

There's a large 'lost property' container at my son's school. It's always overflowing, so every few weeks it gets turned out and the teachers encourage parents to trawl through to identify lost items. The lost property is a sorrowful sight—lots of little heaps of worn and sagging fleeces, tracksuits and jeans, odd socks and gloves, scarves that are so stretched as to look more like string than scarves. It's also an amazing sight! How is it that so many dozens of items can be mislaid, yet nobody misses them? Between the big turn-outs, though, there are times when people go hunting for a particular item. It's intriguing how, as soon as you light upon the thing you are looking for, your whole perception changes. As you catch sight of your missing sweatshirt or T-shirt, it seems somehow different from all the other bits and pieces—not just a limp, sweaty item of lost clothing but the very thing you were looking for! It represents money that will not have to be spent on a replacement, or it may have more sentimental value—a T-shirt from a favourite holiday, for instance. What was lost is now found, and it fills you with satisfaction.

Three of Jesus' stories about being lost and found are traditionally told in Lent. Throughout his Gospel, Luke places a strong emphasis on the marginalised members of society, and the 15th chapter begins with Jesus challenging the Pharisees and scribes who had complained that he was spending too much time with outsiders. 'This fellow welcomes sinners and eats with them,' they say (v. 2, NRSV). The 'lost and found' stories play out the idea of God seeking out lost people, but they do more than just repeat a point: each one develops the idea slightly differently. In the context of our Lenten journey, in which we're seeking to allow our imperfect and incomplete view of God to be brought into clearer focus, it seems to me that there's a connection here. This is a sequence of stories that takes the Pharisees' and scribes' idea of what a religious person ought to be like, and turns it around to ask instead what God is like.

There is no single coin in our currency that's as valuable as the coin in today's story. It wouldn't be worth spending an entire day turning over every piece of paper in your room, going through your clothes and your pockets, turning out your bags and your suitcases, trying to find a mere £2 coin, but the coin in this story was worth a whole day's wages. Not only that, but, as one of ten coins, it was probably the woman's dowry collection, her savings and investment for the future. What might there be in our daily life that has equivalent value to this coin? You could estimate a tenth of a pension fund, or work out roughly how much you earn in a day: it wouldn't be a fortune, but a significant amount of money.

For the sake of argument, imagine you had four £50 notes in your purse or wallet, which you then lost. What would you do? If you're like me, you would begin straight away to try to find it. You'd retrace your steps—go back and look on the last desk you worked at, and rummage through all your pockets and books and papers, trying to find the money. To put it in perspective, it wouldn't necessarily be a matter of life and death if you didn't find it. It might not ruin your life if you lost two hundred pounds, but it would certainly ruin your day. And if you found it—well, again, it wouldn't change the world and it might not dramatically change your life, but it would be a huge relief.

This Lenten story tells us that Jesus understands the daily round of small achievements, of practical worries and anxieties. He knows the stress of a sleepless night when something happens that isn't of world-changing proportions but really matters to *you*. He knows the value of things that matter to ordinary people and, knowing all that, he places the concerns of the kingdom of heaven right there in the everyday.

Heaven rejoices over one person's spiritual rebirth in the same way that this woman is relieved and delighted when she finds her coin. A politician dealing with a national budget will find an error of a few hundred pounds at worst a minor book-keeping inconvenience, but ordinary lives matter to God—each of them, one by one. However small and insignificant we may seem to ourselves, in God's eyes no person gets lost in the multitude.

The kingdom of God, as Jesus tells it, recognises the importance of what is small but personally important; it's made real, most of the time, not at the international level but within the boundaries of everyday existence.

Lost and found (2): the lost sheep

Now the tax collectors and sinners were all drawing near to hear him. And the Pharisees and the scribes grumbled, saying, 'This man receives sinners and eats with them.' So he told them this parable: 'What man of you, having a hundred sheep, if he has lost one of them, does not leave the ninety-nine in the open country, and go after the one that is lost, until he finds it? And when he has found it, he lays it on his shoulders, rejoicing. And when he comes home, he calls together his friends and his neighbours, saying to them, 'Rejoice with me, for I have found my sheep that was lost.' Just so, I tell you, there will be more joy in heaven over one sinner who repents than over ninety-nine righteous persons who need no repentance.

LUKE 15:1–7 (ESV)

Yesterday we read the story of the lost coin, a story about losing something important—not important enough to change the world but enough to make us realise that ordinary people with ordinary lives matter to God. This story of a lost sheep pushes us to think further about what God does with lost things.

I'm not much of a country girl myself—I like the big city, and Cambridge is about as close to rural living as I plan to get—but I have a younger brother who took a career break some years back and worked as a shepherd. He tells me that, contrary to popular belief, sheep are not stupid animals, but they do become quite bewildered and disoriented when they get separated from the group. A lost sheep is a very lost thing indeed: it will not find its own way home, any more than a lost coin will walk back into your purse. The only way to recover a lost sheep is to go out and find it.

There are many forms of spiritual wisdom that offer disciplines and rituals designed to help people find God. Within Christianity, there are encouragements to be active in seeking God: 'Draw near to God,' wrote James (4:8), 'and he will draw near to you.' But underlying this adjuration to open ourselves up to God is the deeper truth that we cannot find God through our own effort. It is God who takes the initiative in salvation, God's grace that draws us towards him, God who runs out to meet us before we have even turned our faces in his direction. Redemption occurs because of God's decisive movement towards us.

The question is often raised, concerning this parable, about the risk that a shepherd takes by leaving his 99 safely herded sheep alone in order to track down just one stray. It's sometimes said that this emphasises how important each person is to God—that God is less interested in the numbers gathered in pews than in the state of each individual soul. What's not so immediately clear from the story, though, is that it was really the shepherd whose safety was at risk, not that of the 99 sheep.

Shepherds didn't usually work alone in first-century Palestine. Remember the shepherds in the nativity story? They were in the fields together, not alone (Luke 2:8). They worked together not only to protect the sheep but to protect themselves as well: there's safety in numbers. So when the shepherd went in search of his missing sheep, the flock would have been watched over by his co-workers. The real risk was to the searching shepherd. Had he met with bandits or fallen down a ravine, he'd probably never have been heard of again, but the lost sheep mattered enough for him to risk life and limb to find it. The point, then, is not the relative value of one lost sheep over 99 safely herded in, but that the shepherd knows his flock and is proactive in caring for each one, even at great cost to himself.

Isaiah's description of God as a shepherd was immortalised in Handel's *Messiah*: 'He shall feed his flock like a shepherd: he shall gather the lambs with his arm, and carry them in his bosom, and shall gently lead those that are with young' (Isaiah 40:11, KJV). The tenderness of the words is intensified by Handel's setting, not as a sentimental image of mother-love, but as a picture of the kind of faithful, determined care that goes beyond mere feelings. Parents care for their children, and carers for ill or aged relatives, and they undoubtedly do so out of love, but many times it is not so much a matter of feeling but of dogged commitment in the face of extreme tiredness. I have never loved anyone more than I love my son but my early memories of motherhood are mostly of slogging through several years of broken nights and grey days with a child who, for a long time, couldn't learn to feed or sleep or talk. I looked after him not because of glowing feelings but from a much deeper sense of care and responsibility. The image of the shepherd risking his life for the sheep is not one of Jesus in a romantic haze of love for his people, but of utter dependability and a determined refusal to give up the search for a soul who is lost in the night.

The lost sheep, then, like the lost coin, gives us some clue as to how we understand our redemption. The lost coin—the missing wallet of notes—was of material significance, and it was a cause for rejoicing when it was found again. Heaven, we are told, has this much joy over individual souls. But God's action in redemption goes further than simply hunting high and low for something valuable that has been mislaid. It's a movement of ultimate personal risk for the sake of something lost almost beyond hope.

The tenor of this story is not only that lost people matter to God as much as lost things matter to us, but that God would, as it were, take any risk to his own safety rather than live without us. Although we may make sacrifices of time and effort in order to attune ourselves to God, the greater sacrifice and initiative always belong to him and not to us. We cannot find our own way into God's presence; only he can carry us there.

Lost and found (3): two lost sons

Then Jesus said, 'There was a man who had two sons. The younger of them said to his father, "Father, give me the share of the property that will belong to me." So he divided his property between them. A few days later the younger son gathered all he had and travelled to a distant country, and there he squandered his property... A severe famine took place throughout that country, and he began to be in need. So he went and hired himself out to one of the citizens of that country, who sent him to his fields to feed the pigs. He would gladly have filled himself with the pods that the pigs were eating; and no one gave him anything. But when he came to himself he said, "How many of my father's hired hands have bread enough and to spare, but here I am dying of hunger! I will get up and go to my father, and I will say to him, 'Father, I have sinned against heaven and before you; I am no longer worthy to be called your son; treat me like one of your hired hands.'" So he set off and went to his father. But while he was still far off, his father saw him and was filled with compassion; he ran and put his arms around him and kissed him. Then the son said to him, "Father, I have sinned against heaven and before you; I am no longer worthy to be called your son." But the father said to his slaves, "Quickly, bring out a robe—the best one—and put it on him; put a ring on his finger and sandals on his feet. And get the fatted calf and kill it, and let us eat and celebrate; for this son of mine was dead and is alive again; he was lost and is found!" And they began to celebrate.

'Now his elder son was in the field... He called one of the slaves and asked what was going on. He replied, "Your brother has come, and your father has killed the fatted calf..." Then he became angry and refused to go in. His father came out and began to plead with him. But he answered his father, "Listen! For all these years I have been working like a slave for you... yet you have never given me even a young goat so that I might celebrate with my friends. But when this son of yours came back, who has devoured your property with prostitutes, you killed the fatted calf for him!" Then the father said to him, "Son, you are always with me, and all that is mine is yours. But we had to celebrate and rejoice, because this brother of yours was dead and has come to life; he was lost and has been found."'

LUKE 15:11–32 (ABRIDGED)

The third lost-and-found story in Luke's Gospel is the prodigal son. To be prodigal means to be generous to the point of being a reckless spendthrift, to give without concern for whether the gift will be wasted. It's a term that obviously fits the younger son well. All his actions from the very beginning of the story are outrageous. Within his culture, to ask for his inheritance early was tantamount to wishing his father was already dead. It was also unfair on the older brother, for, by dividing the family fortune in two, the younger brother simply walked away with his share in realised assets, leaving his father and brother to manage a vastly reduced estate. To make matters worse, having taken all that money out of the estate, he squandered it. Eventually he found himself flat broke, discovered that his friends were only fair-weather friends, and had to take the lowliest of jobs, keeping pigs. He was so hungry that he would gladly have eaten the pigs' food—something especially repugnant for a Jew—but he was denied even this, which sent the clear message that he was of less value than a pig.

The bad behaviour and shocking wastefulness of the son are beyond doubt, but I think there's a bit of a twist in the tale. I notice that the son wastes his money by spending it all not just on himself but on his wayward friends. Have you ever stopped to wonder where he learned to be quite so outrageously, unquestioningly open-handed? You could argue that his father should have been sterner, more intent on teaching his young son self-discipline; that instead of parting so easily with the inheritance, he should have pulled his son into line. But the father himself is outrageously generous and is far more interested in building a relationship with his two sons than looking after the family wealth. Dividing the property for his son was, in itself, lavish to the point of recklessness, carried out in the full knowledge that the resources would probably be wasted. Yet it seems that he would rather see his money trickling down through the cracks than risk such anger and resentment brewing in his son that he would lose him for ever.

When the son, without a second thought, is over-generous towards his profligate friends, I can't help thinking that he's a chip off the old block. He has learnt that money is important only insofar as it supports friendship, kinship and love. Where did he learn that lesson? From his prodigal father, perhaps?

When the son finally heads home, his father is not only waiting for him but actually runs out to meet him. In that culture, dignified men did not run to meet their guests, but this father ran to his son, so overflowing with love for him that he could not bear to be without him. Danish theologian Søren

Kierkegaard pointed out that what connects the three lost-and-found stories is this action of going out to look. The woman doesn't just wait for the coin to reappear but turns the house upside down until she finds it, the shepherd leaves the 99 to go and find the one, and the father doesn't wait for his son to come home but goes out to find him. We don't have to come knocking on heaven's door after all: long before heaven comes into view, God is already halfway down the road to show us in.

What's interesting, though, is that the father goes out looking in this way not just once but twice, for there are two lost sons in this story. The older son never left home but he's lost in such a sea of resentment that, when the party begins, he stays outside, sulking. He has good reason to feel put upon, of course. His younger brother, having wasted his own half of the inheritance, is now enjoying a huge, expensive feast which is being paid for out of the elder brother's share of the estate. His prodigal father is (dare we think it?) even worse than his younger brother. He's wasteful, excessive in his generosity.

The character of the older brother seems to be a direct reply to the Pharisees and scribes, in response to whose criticism Jesus told the three lost-and-found stories. The older brother is the upstanding but critical Pharisee who not only knew the religious rules but actually kept them all. In our context, the older brother is the upright, devoutly religious person, the respected yet resentful churchgoer. He is the ultimate insider, someone who controls the committee meetings, holds the keys, keeps the books, reads the lessons, leads the intercessions. But in the story it turns out that he is not inside at all, but outside, because even though we may live on the property, a cold heart removes us from God's presence into a darkness of our own making. No matter how perfectly we keep our religion, it's our heart that places us inside or outside God's presence.

The father is no more fazed by his over-responsible, self-righteous son than he is by the repentant good-time boy. Out goes the father once again, not satisfied until all his children are by his side, not merely sharing an inheritance but rejoicing in being together. Prodigal son—or prodigal father? Two lost sons—or one searching father? In the end, the story isn't so much about one lost son or two but about the unstinting generosity of God, whose love casts reason, convention and dignity aside.

Stormy weather

On that day, when evening had come, he said to them, 'Let us go across to the other side.' And leaving the crowd behind, they took him with them in the boat, just as he was. Other boats were with him. A great gale arose, and the waves beat into the boat, so that the boat was already being swamped. But he was in the stern, asleep on the cushion; and they woke him up and said to him, 'Teacher, do you not care that we are perishing?' He woke up and rebuked the wind, and said to the sea, 'Peace! Be still!' Then the wind ceased, and there was a dead calm. He said to them, 'Why are you afraid? Have you still no faith?'

MARK 4:35–40

In England you're never more than 74 miles from the sea-shore, and it really is possible, wherever you live, to get to the coast and back in a day. For me it's a couple of hours' drive to a coastline that is particularly lovely in the winter, its bleak mudflats somehow seeming specially suited to a winter frost. I love the sea. There's something about the salty smell and the beating of the waves on the shore that is therapeutic. Perhaps, too, there's something about that liminal space between land and sea that opens up a sense of possibility. On a beach, our defined, landlocked life encounters the edge of an uncontrollable freedom. Maybe that's why the seashore seems to restore perspective: it reminds us that we're not as 'in control' as we think we are, and certainly not nearly as important. Yet, therapeutic though it may be, the wildness of the sea is not to be underestimated.

A couple of decades ago, I lived for a year and a half in a small town on the edge of a Norwegian fjord. A few weeks into my visit, some of the locals decided that I should be properly initiated into an understanding of the local industries, and that began with a fishing trip. We set out on smooth seas that glinted as the sun caught the movement of the water beneath the boat. We stowed our waterproofs and sweaters, as it was warm and dry, a very promising day. On the way out, I was shown various fishing techniques: this trip had in part been set up for my education, so they were going to let me fish with a line on one side of the boat. Eventually we got everything set up and various lines and nets were spread about the place. After some hours, quite suddenly the sun faded and the clouds began to gather, and the guy in charge announced that we should pack up urgently and head for home. Within the space of a few minutes, the calm sea turned choppy, the clouds grew dark and forbidding, the light dropped dramatically, and the rain began to come down in sheets until the horizon blurred and you couldn't tell where the rain ended and the sea began.

The fishermen went into emergency mode, pushing me down in the middle of the boat and tying me on to something with big ropes. Then they tied themselves together and on to the boat, and we began to head towards land, riding over enormous waves. Too numb to feel fear, I remember willing the storm to subside and trying to find a point of focus to stop my head from spinning into uncontrollable nausea. A long time later, when we came in to land, the quayside was lined with people waiting with blankets and hot drinks. As I warmed up, I began to realise that we had been in real danger. I also registered that the wives on the quayside waited there pretty often, with their arms full of blankets and their hearts in their mouths. For the first time I grasped how real the 'perils of the deep' are, and how swiftly you can go from a happy day on the water to life-threatening danger.

Quite a few of Jesus' disciples were experienced fishermen who worked on the Sea of Galilee, a stretch of water that usually looks idyllic in its mirror-like calm but can blow up into a violent storm in a matter of minutes. It is actually a huge lake—14 miles long, three miles wide at the narrow point, and seven miles across at the widest place. On a calm day it doesn't take long for experienced fishermen to cross it, but in a fierce storm a stretch of water that size is a dangerous place to be.

Today's story is the first of two that Mark tells about Jesus helping the disciples during a storm. He describes the disciples' fear and distress and their bewilderment at Jesus' remaining asleep. They might well have been amazed that he could sleep through a storm of that magnitude but Mark tells us they were mystified that he wasn't doing anything to help, while they were at the end of their tether, their lives in danger.

His apparent lack of care for his disciples, sleeping while the storm raged, is a good picture of one of the most difficult theological issues for modern Western people. The problem of suffering is one of the biggest stumbling blocks to faith. Why does God seem to do nothing, to be curiously absent just when we need him most, to be asleep when the storm is raging? We've already seen that Job threw a torrent of questions at God in the midst of his suffering, and yet in the end was satisfied not so much by receiving an answer to his questions but by meeting God. In a way, the same thing happens here with the disciples. Jesus never explains why he slept through the storm and, far from sympathising with their distress, he gives them something of a rebuke for having been afraid in the first place. The mystery is answered only in this—that God is present with them through the suffering.

Not all stories of suffering have a happy ending; we can't assume that if we have faith in God everything will turn out right. In Job's story, God didn't turn back the clock and restore what Job had lost, but he did restore him to peace and prosperity and a new future. In this story, we do see Jesus restoring peace and bringing his disciples safely to shore. It would be over-reading the story to interpret this as a promise that God will take care of all our troubles for us, but we can learn that he is with us in difficulties, brings peace in the storm and guides us into the future.

Another storm

Immediately [Jesus] made his disciples get into the boat and go on ahead to the other side, to Bethsaida, while he dismissed the crowd. After saying farewell to them, he went up on the mountain to pray.

When evening came, the boat was out on the lake, and he was alone on the land. When he saw that they were straining at the oars against an adverse wind, he came towards them early in the morning, walking on the lake. He intended to pass them by. But when they saw him walking on the lake, they thought it was a ghost and cried out; for they all saw him and were terrified. But immediately he spoke to them and said, 'Take heart, it is I; do not be afraid.' Then he got into the boat with them and the wind ceased. And they were utterly astounded, for they did not understand about the loaves, but their hearts were hardened.

MARK 6:45–52

Yesterday we read a story in which the disciples were full of fear during a storm on the lake, and, although Jesus was with them in the boat, he was asleep and not helping them in their distress. In this second story there is another storm, perhaps not as fierce as the first one, since the disciples are not reported as being fearful, although perhaps they were simply absorbed with the task of bringing the boat through the storm. John's version of the story tells us that they rowed three-and-a-half miles through heavy wind and waves before Jesus came to them (John 6:19). Mark simply tells us that the boat was on the sea in the evening, and it was early morning—dawn, perhaps—by the time Jesus walked across the sea towards them. Again, this suggests several hours of rowing against rough seas without making much progress.

The separation of Jesus from the disciples in the story is amplified by the symbolism of sea and mountains. Jesus left the disciples to go alone up the mountain, which, as we have seen, usually symbolises the place of God's revelation. Meanwhile, the disciples departed across the sea, which is often used in the Bible to represent the chaos and wickedness of humanity apart from God (hence 'the sea was no more' in John's vision of the new heaven and earth in Revelation 21:1). Here, the disciples' physical separation from Jesus parallels a much deeper isolation—the alienation of people from themselves and from God.

Given that the disciples had been battling this particular storm all through the night, you might expect that the sight of Jesus approaching would be a comfort and a relief. As in a number of passages in the Gospels, though, there is a disruption of normal perception as the disciples meet Jesus but simply don't recognise him, in the same way as Mary on Easter morning (John 20:11–18) and the disciples on the road to Emmaus (Luke 24:13–35). These disciples are battling the storm, longing for Jesus to help them, and yet, when he does appear before them, they don't realise it's him. Far from calming them down, his appearance actually increases their fear, for now they think that on top of everything else they have a ghost to deal with. Stress and anxiety often serve to impair our perception and our judgment. Sometimes, if we're cast adrift in difficult and alienating circumstances and have to work hard just to stay afloat, we become incapable of recognising hope when it appears on our horizon. The very thing that's thrown to us as a lifeline appears at first to make matters worse.

This is one of only a few Gospel stories in which Jesus seems to step completely outside his human limitations. Each of the Gospel writers tells us that Jesus strode across the water; John goes even further and claims that as soon as Jesus was in the boat, they were miraculously transported to the other side of the lake (6:21). It's inconclusive, and not even particularly interesting, to speculate on whether the miracle is believable. Miracles are, by nature, implausible, and arguing about whether they really happened or whether there is a rational explanation for them is a cul-de-sac: you can't prove it decisively one way or the other. What's more interesting about this ghostly appearance is that it gives Mark, who doesn't tell any resurrection stories, an opportunity to portray Jesus in an unrecognisable superhuman form. The other three Gospels convey this sense of human–divine mystery through the resurrection appearances. John tells of Jesus suddenly appearing inside a room where the doors are locked (20:19); Luke also tells of a resurrection appearance where Jesus materialises in a superhuman way, and yet, when he does so, it is with his familiar, human body (24:36–39); and Matthew tells of the mixture of joy and fear that the women experienced when first they met angels in the empty tomb and then Jesus himself suddenly appeared (28:1–10).

Here in Mark, the ghostly apparition of Jesus walking across the water strikes fear into the hearts of these tough fishermen. He doesn't look like the Jesus they know; even though they have been bravely facing down wind and waves for several hours, this strange phenomenon is too much for them and their fear is palpable. The point of recognition comes at Jesus' words, 'It is I…' (v. 50). Sometimes the English translation misses the point here, that Jesus is saying something more than just 'It's me.' The Greek reads *ego eimi* ('I am'), which clearly connects us back to the stories of naming and identity from Exodus. 'Who am I...?' asked Moses, but God's reply inverted Moses' question: 'I am who I am... You shall say... "*I am* has sent me to you"' (Exodus 3:11,14).

Even then, Mark seems to suggest that the disciples did not really grasp what was happening. Throughout his Gospel, Mark paints a picture of the disciples as being very slow on the uptake, perhaps as a way of pushing his readers to ask themselves who *they* think Jesus is. The disciples had not understood the significance of what happened earlier in the day when Jesus fed 5000 people with just a few loaves and fish, and even now, when they see him switching between divine and human capabilities, they seem unable to take it in.

The story highlights the fact that in Jesus the stark distinction between human and divine is in some way brought together. The ghostly Jesus outside the boat represents the unknowable, unrecognisable presence of God—the God who cannot be grasped and who creates a storm of fear in our souls—but once he steps into the boat he is recognisable to us, and everything becomes calm and still. We can't even begin to know God until we accept the paradoxical nature of the encounter—that he is, on the one hand, limitless and unknowable, and, on the other hand, made known to us in the practical realities of everyday life. We only begin to understand when we know that, in fact, we will never understand. The knowable and the unknowable have to be held in tension.

Walking on water

[Jesus] made the disciples get into the boat and go on ahead to the other side, while he dismissed the crowds. And after he had dismissed the crowds, he went up the mountain by himself to pray. When evening came, he was there alone, but by this time the boat, battered by the waves, was far from the land, for the wind was against them. And early in the morning he came walking towards them on the lake. But when the disciples saw him walking on the lake, they were terrified, saying, 'It is a ghost!' And they cried out in fear. But immediately Jesus spoke to them and said, 'Take heart, it is I; do not be afraid.'

Peter answered him, 'Lord, if it is you, command me to come to you on the water.' He said, 'Come.' So Peter got out of the boat, started walking on the water, and came towards Jesus. But when he noticed the strong wind, he became frightened, and beginning to sink, he cried out, 'Lord, save me!' Jesus immediately reached out his hand and caught him, saying to him, 'You of little faith, why did you doubt?' When they got into the boat, the wind ceased. And those in the boat worshipped him, saying, 'Truly you are the Son of God.'

MATTHEW 14:22–33

If you think you're having déjà vu—no, this is not a misprint. It is indeed the same story we read yesterday, but this time told by Matthew. As is so often the case with the four Gospels, we hear different threads in the story when it is told by somebody else. I'm highly resistant to the idea that we should amalgamate the accounts given by the different Gospel writers. By changing the order of events or presenting them from another point of view, the individual writers subtly shift the sense and purpose of the story.

Matthew's tale has a lot in common with Mark's version: in fact, most scholars believe that Matthew and Luke borrowed extensively from Mark's Gospel when they wrote their own. Here, Matthew retells Mark's story but, by adding the account of Peter's response, Matthew takes the story off in another direction and emphasises the effect of one man's faith on the group as a whole.

I love the way that Peter is prepared to go out on a limb. Still uncertain as to whether it really is Jesus he can see, he's prepared to take the risk that it is. You might call this a leap of faith—a term coined by Søren Kierkegaard. We often think of a leap of faith as a jump into the complete unknown but, the way Kierkegaard describes it, it is more like Peter's action here. It's an attempt to make a connection across the inevitable gaps of logic in any system of thought. Kierkegaard's point is that it's futile to try to bridge every gap in logic; instead, we have to make the connections with a leap of faith. This is not irrational, but, because faith concerns that which can be neither proved nor disproved, it is always uncertain. A leap of faith is not so much an act of madness as a calculated risk, not knowing for certain what the end will look like but with a reasonable belief that, despite the mystery that God is to us, God will nonetheless meet us. So it proved for Peter.

It's often said about this story that if you want to walk on water, you have to get out of the boat. It's true that only Peter got to walk on water, but the others did meet and worship Jesus, and they were all rescued. Because we live in a society that focuses on the individual, we tend to read the scriptures as if they are a template for an individual's relationship with God rather than stories about the people of God. In fact, there is no suggestion of condemnation here upon the other disciples: Jesus did not command them all to walk on the water but he brought them all to safety, and the end of the story was not an object lesson for the other disciples about the faith they might have had. In point of fact, the only person who got rebuked was Peter, for wavering over the faith he was trying to muster.

We don't all react to God in the same way. Some of us are activists and others contemplatives; some quick to take a risk while others move more cautiously and count the cost— something that is elsewhere commended by Jesus. To compare the disciples critically and suggest that we should all be like Peter is a highly individualistic reading of the story. What was the response of the group? They all saw Jesus and most of them, presumably, kept the boat afloat while Peter was having his walking-on-water experience. The result of Peter's action in this story was not just that he gained a deeper personal relationship with Jesus; rather, the whole group of disciples ended up safe in the boat, in calm waters, worshipping Jesus.

Should I stay or should I go?

[Jesus and the disciples] came to the other side of the lake, to the country of the Gerasenes. And when he had stepped out of the boat, immediately a man out of the tombs with an unclean spirit met him. He lived among the tombs; and no one could restrain him any more, even with a chain; for he had often been restrained with shackles and chains, but the chains he wrenched apart, and the shackles he broke in pieces; and no one had the strength to subdue him. Night and day among the tombs and on the mountains he was always howling and bruising himself with stones. When he saw Jesus from a distance, he ran and bowed down before him; and he shouted at the top of his voice, 'What have you to do with me, Jesus, Son of the Most High God? I adjure you by God, do not torment me.' For he had said to him, 'Come out of the man, you unclean spirit!' Then Jesus asked him, 'What is your name?' He replied, 'My name is Legion; for we are many.' He begged him earnestly not to send them out of the country. Now there on the hillside a great herd of swine was feeding; and the unclean spirits begged him, 'Send us into the swine; let us enter them.' So he gave them permission. And the unclean spirits came out and entered the swine; and the herd, numbering about two thousand, rushed down the steep bank into the lake, and were drowned in the lake.

The swineherds ran off and told it in the city and in the country. Then people came to see what it was that had happened. They came to Jesus and saw the demoniac sitting there, clothed and in his right mind, the very man who had had the legion; and they were afraid. Those who had seen what had happened to the demoniac and to the swine reported it. Then they began to beg Jesus to leave their neighbourhood. As he was getting into the boat, the man who had been possessed by demons begged him that he might be with him. But Jesus refused, and said to him, 'Go home to your friends, and tell them how much the Lord has done for you, and what mercy he has shown you.' And he went away and began to proclaim in the Decapolis how much Jesus had done for him; and everyone was amazed.

MARK 5:1–20

Stories about demons are hard to interpret in the 21st century. It's rare now to hear maladies talked about in terms of evil spirits. Increased understanding of the physical workings of the brain and of human psychology have given us much more refined ways of analysing the human mind and, reading the story of the Gerasene man from our perspective, we are bound to think that he was ill rather than 'possessed'. Mental illness, though, is just as much a stigma in our society as evil spirits ever were in earlier times. It's often true that human sympathy is still sadly lacking, and those who suffer various forms of distress or mental disorder are regarded with fear and suspicion.

If we leave aside the puzzling issue of demons and diagnoses, another interesting theme comes into view—the way in which this man's disorder affected his relationship to his community. It's clear that Legion was ill, in deep personal distress, and living in social isolation outside the boundaries of the settlement. His friends and neighbours had, apparently, done their best to restrain him, even tying him down with chains, but his overpowering and disordered strength made it impossible for them to control him. So they gave up trying to help, and he ended up wandering among the graves, his violence turned against himself, howling and wounding himself physically in the vain attempt to relieve his mental anguish. By the time Jesus arrived on the scene, poor Legion's existence was, as the haunting metaphor of the tombs suggests, a living death.

There are many Bible stories that show Jesus meeting and healing society's outsiders, but often it was difficult for people to get to Jesus when he was surrounded by huge crowds. Sometimes Jesus deliberately went out of his way to meet the disadvantaged, such as Bartimaeus the blind man (Mark 10:46–49). Sometimes other people found ways of cutting through the crowds: remember the four men who lowered their friend through the roof of a house (Mark 2:1–5)? I cannot imagine that Legion would have been able to cope with pushing his way through a crowd to meet Jesus, like the woman with the haemorrhage did (Luke 8:44–45). In the land of the Gerasenes, though, Jesus was not known, and so, as he came ashore, it was precisely by virtue of the fact that Legion was an outsider that he met Jesus first. Sometimes social disadvantage seems to be the very factor that opens people up to God.

There was a huge conflict as Legion approached Jesus, however. Perhaps in something of an echo of Moses approaching the presence of God in the burning bush (Exodus 3:2–5), Legion was powerfully attracted to this source of light and life, but at the same time the overwhelming purity and holiness of Jesus repelled him. Jesus embodied everything that he couldn't find within himself—stillness, beauty, order, intense vitality—but in his damaged and disordered state Legion couldn't bear to come too close.

This kind of internal conflict often occurs when we're faced with a shift into a different mode of living. Those who have suffered from a lengthy illness will know that the prospect of returning to normal life is full of hope, but there is also a degree of fear. The routines and identity that come with being ill may not have been welcome, but they can become a place of security. Returning to health and the responsibilities of life after a period of debilitation can be daunting. Similar feelings of conflict can come when one period in our lives comes to an end and it's time for a complete change of gear—starting work after leaving college, going back to work after maternity leave, or working out what to do in retirement. Legion's reaction to Jesus was an extreme form of this conflict.

After the healing, the end of the story plays out like a reversal of the beginning. So ill and out of control that he was described as evil, Legion started out unable to tolerate the perfection and holiness of Jesus. The story closes with him healed and at peace with himself, but now he cannot bear to let Jesus go. Jesus, though, refuses to take Legion with him, despite the fact that he had called other disciples to leave everything behind and follow him. Why was it important for Legion to stay? This takes us back to the theme of Legion's relationship with other people, and how significant that was not only for his own well-being but for the whole community.

Jesus told him to go and tell his friends what had happened. It's perhaps significant that the word 'friends' is used here, given the loneliness Legion seems to have endured. We're told that his neighbours were afraid of the newly healthy man. Perhaps they, too, had an internal conflict—wanting to believe that healing was possible but afraid of coming too close unless they got involved again in something they couldn't cope with.

Of course we should maintain a proper level of caution for the safety of our communities, but perhaps Jesus saw that in this case the people of the Decapolis (the ten towns) needed to know that healing and restoration are possible. Perhaps, too, he saw that Legion's healing would be completed only by discovering that his neighbours, who had given up on him and feared him, could once again become his friends.

By staying in his own town and allowing people to see his transformation, Legion became the 'before-and-after' picture, the evidence that redemption really is possible, even for supposedly hopeless cases.

Questions for reflection

- What does it mean for God to 'go out' and find people? How does this affect our understanding of our own relationship to God? How does it affect our understanding of mission?
- Are there ways in which God has appeared in my life and I haven't recognised him—perhaps through a situation I've found myself in or a person I have met?
- How might healing (our own or someone else's) affect our community? Could our stories be a source of hope to other people? Does someone recovering from illness or addiction need our acceptance? Might they be able to teach us something about love?

Changing communities

Mid-Lent breakfast

While [Jesus] was still speaking to the crowds, his mother and his brothers were standing outside, wanting to speak to him. Someone told him, 'Look, your mother and your brothers are standing outside, wanting to speak to you.' But to the one who had told him this, Jesus replied, 'Who is my mother, and who are my brothers?' And pointing to his disciples, he said, 'Here are my mother and my brothers! For whoever does the will of my Father in heaven is my brother and sister and mother.'

MATTHEW 12:46–50

In 16th-century Britain, the fourth Sunday of Lent was called Refreshment Sunday. All the Lent rules were relaxed and the Church expected people to return to their 'mother' church or cathedral for that day's service. The day became known as Mothering Sunday, not through association with mothers but because of the journey made to the 'mother' church. In an age when children as young as ten left home to take up work or apprenticeships elsewhere, this was often the only day in the year when whole families would be reunited. By the 17th century it had become a public holiday, when servants and apprentices were given the day off so that they could fulfil their duties to the Church. They often stopped to pick flowers along the way and some brought with them a special cake made from fine wheat flour called simila, which has evolved into the simnel cake, decorated with eleven balls of marzipan representing eleven of the twelve disciples (excluding Judas Iscariot). The tradition of keeping Mothering Sunday was strengthened in the 19th century when those in domestic service were allowed to return to their own communities, as they would not be at home for Easter.

The different threads of the history of the fourth Sunday in Lent give us a way to revisit what has become something of a liturgical anomaly. Over the past few decades, Mothering Sunday has gradually been recast as Mothers' Day, a move that has grown out of consumerism more than theology. Turning Mothering Sunday into Mothers' Day has almost completely eclipsed the original meaning of the day so that, for example, the current Church of England liturgy for the day includes prayers of thanks for motherhood and a pause for flowers to be distributed to mothers.

While, on the surface, it seems a nice idea to spend a whole Sunday celebrating mothers, it has a complicated flipside. Why only mothers? Why not fathers, grandparents, children, aunts and uncles, siblings, single people, childless people and more? The romanticisation of the mother–child relationship is full of fraught overtones: what does it say to women who are not mothers? Are we suggesting that their contribution to the world is somehow less valuable, less worth a celebratory day? The new focus on Mothers' Day comes with barbs for those who are childless but not by choice, for those who are infertile or have suffered miscarriages, for women whose children have died or are estranged, or for single or widowed fathers.

Some years ago I suffered an early miscarriage and, given the brevity of the experience, I was almost surprised to find that, while the world continued to turn unawares, I was quite washed away with grief. One of my closest friends at the time was a woman older than me who had longed for children but never been able to have any herself. Rather than talking interminably about my situation, she simply checked up on me regularly to make sure that I was eating and sleeping properly and getting out and having some fun.

After a few weeks, Mothering Sunday loomed on the horizon. I began to tell myself that I would be fine by then, that I would think happy thoughts and get through the services without a worry. Then my friend called. 'I've booked a cottage in the country,' she announced. 'Inform your church that you're taking the weekend off. You need to come away with us. We will not spend a single moment thinking about mothers and children; we will have a mid-Lent feast that focuses on the family of the Church. That's you and me, kid.'

She was so right. The last thing I (and the six other men and women she had invited away for the weekend) needed was to dwell on our griefs and have them aggravated by children with bunches of flowers and the vaguely implied message that real women are mothers. Instead, we cooked and talked, laughed and sang, prayed and gave thanks for community and friendship and life in all its fullness. I came home at the end of the weekend with hope reborn in my heart that life would go on.

Jesus' words concerning his mother and family are among his 'hard sayings': they sound rude and lacking in compassion, hard to reconcile with the Jesus who seems to care about everyone everywhere. Yet maybe, rather than rejecting his own mother and brothers, he is calling us to broaden our vision of community so that we encompass those who cannot retreat to tight-knit family units of their own.

I think it would be worth putting serious thought into reshaping today's feast so that family life is placed firmly within the wider context of the community of Mother Church.

We may fear an outcry if we shifted the focus of this mid-Lent feast away from the idea of Mothers' Day, but our concept of family life will be sad and inadequate if we allow it to be constructed for us by advertising campaigns and the greeting card industry. If, like Jesus, we have the courage to embrace a much wider concept of community than our nuclear family, we too might find that we don't have to accept our culture's myths about families.

'You feed them...'

The day was drawing to a close, and the twelve came to Jesus and said, 'Send the crowd away, so that they may go into the surrounding villages and countryside, to lodge and get provisions; for we are here in a deserted place.' But he said to them, 'You give them something to eat.' They said, 'We have no more than five loaves and two fish—unless we are to go and buy food for all these people.' For there were about five thousand men. And he said to his disciples, 'Make them sit down in groups of about fifty each.' They did so and made them all sit down. And taking the five loaves and the two fish, he looked up to heaven, and blessed and broke them, and gave them to the disciples to set before the crowd. And all ate and were filled. What was left over was gathered up, twelve baskets of broken pieces.

LUKE 9:12–17

Today, after the mid-Lent feast, the Lent discipline is resumed. Before we leave it behind, though, let's pause for a few minutes with one of the traditional readings for the fourth Sunday of Lent, and see what it has to tell us about feasting and fasting.

Lent has never been kept as a non-stop endurance test from Ash Wednesday until Easter morning, but has always been broken up by a number of feast days. In some corners of the

Church, the six Sundays of Lent are celebrated as mini-Easters (this is also one answer to the frequently asked question as to why Lent is supposed to be a 40-day fast, when it is in fact 46 days long). Most cultures that celebrate Lent also have some kind of mid-Lent feast, which, as we noted yesterday, is known in English culture as Mothering Sunday. In French-speaking countries, the *Mi-Carême* or mid-Lent day is celebrated on the fourth Thursday of Lent, when mummers go from house to house dressed in folk costumes.

In the Catholic Church, the fourth Sunday of Lent is called Laetare Sunday because the opening words of the Latin Mass are '*Laetare, Jerusalem*', meaning 'Rejoice, Jerusalem'. Another name for it is Rose Sunday, because roses crafted from pure gold and then blessed by the Pope used to be sent to important churches or chapels, or as a mark of esteem to kings or queens who were loyal Catholics. Another story (probably apocryphal) is that, one Laetare Sunday, the Pope saw a young nun who was looking very downcast and worn out from her fasting. In order to lift her spirits, the story goes, the Pope gave her a pink rose and, from that day onward, instead of Lenten purple vestments, the liturgical colour for the mid-Lent feast has been pink. Whether the story is true or not, it is the case that in many churches the priest will wear pink vestments, both on the middle Sunday of Lent and on Gaudete Sunday, the middle Sunday of Advent.

There are some stoical types who regard breaking the fast as cheating! But the practice of breaking the fast at mid-Lent reinforces the theological undercurrents about why the fast is made in the first place. Four weeks in, we may forget that Lent is not a means of saving or improving ourselves; conversely, we may be doing so badly at our fast that we begin to believe we could lose God's favour. Breaking the fast reminds us that, despite the relative success or failure of our willpower, it is ultimately by grace that we are saved, and not through our own effort.

Before the Protestant Reformation, the fourth Sunday of Lent was celebrated as the anniversary of one of the most famous feasts ever—the feeding of the five thousand. It's a haunting image: huge crowds followed Jesus far out into the wilderness and, as the day wore on, the disciples became worried about the number of people and the fact that they had no way of feeding them. We can only wonder at their reasons. Perhaps they were genuinely concerned that the people were hungry and tired, or perhaps they themselves were hungry and tired and wanted a break. Perhaps they had begun to worry that they had a crowd-control problem on their hands. In any case, Jesus' reply is intriguing—not 'Don't worry, I'll feed them' but 'You feed them: you give them something to eat.' Sometimes in the telling of the story we focus on how Jesus saved the day by blessing and multiplying the food, and we forget that his intention was for the disciples to feed the people. Maybe, when we're concerned with the needs of the world, we need to remember Jesus' words: 'You feed them.'

One December, when I was serving as Chaplain to King's College, Cambridge, I was rushed off my feet in the midst of all the activity surrounding the TV and radio broadcasts of the Festival of Nine Lessons and Carols. One afternoon, there was a knock at my study door and in walked an elegant and studious young woman. She was not a Christian but she had come to seek my help on a problem that was vexing her deeply. Every evening, she told me, there was a mass of surplus food thrown away from the kitchens at Kings—and every evening, not 500 yards from the College, there was a stall where a local charity sought to provide hot food for the many homeless people who sleep on the streets of Cambridge. She could not bear to see the mismatch between our surplus wealth and their need, and wanted to know what could be done. What little she knew of Christianity was that Christians care for the poor, and consequently, in her eyes, I was the obvious person to sort this issue out.

The obligations of Christmas services and the demands of broadcasting deadlines were weighing heavily on me at the time, but what weighed heavier was the preference of the gospel for the poor. No one who takes the gospel seriously could possibly ignore such a request, so together we set about bringing her vision into reality.

We rapidly discovered that there were endless health and safety regulations which meant we could not simply take our surplus food up to the Market Square and feed the hungry. But where there's a will there's a way, and, with the help of a few more students who caught the vision, we found ways around the various obstacles. With a rota of willing helpers we were soon making twice-weekly trips to donate our surplus food from the kitchens to the charity stall.

'You feed them'—not just spiritually; not just with marvellous liturgies and wonderful music, but feeding real, hungry people with real, warm food. It sometimes seems impossible, caught up as we are in our busy lives, to find a way to answer this call. Perhaps all it takes is a little imagination, a little determination and the willingness to spot the opportunity when it arises.

The untouchables

On the way to Jerusalem Jesus was going through the region between Samaria and Galilee. As he entered a village, ten lepers approached him. Keeping their distance, they called out, saying, 'Jesus, Master, have mercy on us!' When he saw them, he said to them, 'Go and show yourselves to the priests.' And as they went, they were made clean. Then one of them, when he saw that he was healed, turned back, praising God with a loud voice. He prostrated himself at Jesus' feet and thanked him. And he was a Samaritan. Then Jesus asked, 'Were not ten made clean? But the other nine, where are they? Was none of them found to return and give praise to God except this foreigner?' Then he said to him, 'Get up and go on your way; your faith has made you well.'
LUKE 17:11–19

Some years ago, I worked in central London with a mission organisation that worked among those living on the streets. For most of them, all we could offer was food, clean clothes and a listening ear, but every now and then we met someone who wanted to find a new life. For people like this, we ran a halfway house with a simple rule of life, where we could take in a few at a time to relearn the basic skills of living indoors. This may not sound difficult, but for people who have grown accustomed to life on the streets it represents a huge challenge. Some of those who came to join us managed the long, difficult process of reintegration, but more than half gave up and later returned to their hard but autonomous life on the streets.

Like most of those who work in missions, I started out with an idea of what I had to offer the world, but living among people whom many consider 'untouchable', I quickly discovered that I had more to learn than I had to give. One thing that made a deep impression on me was the way people on the margins reinvent their social values. On regular visits to a little community under a viaduct near the famous Portobello Road market, I met two men who had a gruff but loyal friendship, short on conversation but long on mutual care. One was an aristocrat who had been educated at one of the finest universities in the land and then inherited a huge country estate. Eventually, under extreme pressure, he had abandoned his fortune, and he now walked the streets with just a few possessions in a supermarket trolley, his cut-glass accent being the only hint of where he'd come from. His friend was a working-class man from the tenements in the poorest area of Glasgow, who had dropped out of the education system in his early teens and come to London to seek his fortune. The likelihood of these men becoming close friends in normal society was slim, but in the community under the viaduct the Scotsman and the English Lord found that their differences were immaterial compared to their common struggle to survive on the streets in a cold climate.

Luke tells us about another community that lived on the margins. Before the advent of modern medicine, there were colonies of lepers beyond the boundaries of most towns, where society kept them for fear of contagion. The ten lepers in Luke's story, however, hoped against hope for healing from the dread disease that had destroyed their bodies and consumed their souls. When they heard that Jesus the miracle worker was nearby, they came as close as they dared and called out for healing.

It's a well-known story: Jesus told them to go to the priests. As they were going they found they had been healed, but only one of them returned to say 'thank you'. Often we focus on the one who came back as an illustration of healing, faith, worship and salvation in the life of the individual, but there's an equally interesting undercurrent to the story. Why did Jesus send them to the priests? Why not just heal them on the spot? I think the answer has to do with prejudice, and the way we exclude people from society.

In first-century Israel, when someone had leprosy they were not only confirmed as having the disease, but were also declared ritually unclean by the priests, which placed them outside the community. By sending the ten back to the priests, Jesus raised the possibility that they would be not only healed but also declared ritually pure, which was essential if they were to reintegrate into society. The twist in the tale is that this particular leper colony was near a village on the border between Galilee and Samaria, communities that were deeply and acrimoniously divided. Jews considered all Samaritans ritually unclean and would travel miles out of their way to avoid having any contact with them.

Stigmatisation is a great leveller and, while they were ill, the ten lepers had discovered that which side of the border you were from meant nothing if you had leprosy. Like my friends under the viaduct, whose differences of class and education were wiped away by the taboo of homelessness, these ten lepers had all become untouchables and had forged their own community on the margins. Once they were healed, though, the old divisions kicked into play again. Ten were healed but only nine would be accepted; the tenth would always be unclean, not because he was a leper but because he was a

Samaritan. He knew that the obstacles to his joining society on the Galilean side of the border ran far deeper than his leprosy. Perhaps it's precisely for this reason that he didn't bother with the priests but turned back to find Jesus.

It was only to the Samaritan that Jesus said, 'Your faith has made you well.' Maybe Jesus was talking about a different kind of wellness. Maybe he meant that deep-seated human divisions are a much more serious malady even than leprosy, that our souls can be far sicker than our bodies and yet most of us do nothing to heal them. Maybe he wasn't commenting on the attitude of the nine who didn't return as much as on the system that would accept them but reject the Samaritan.

We'll never know exactly what Jesus meant but the challenge to our concept of the gospel, and faith and healing, is that they are not merely gifts for the individual; they bring with them consequences and responsibilities. Jesus healed with compassion and generosity but he also consistently drew people's attention away from their own problems to the bigger picture. We are not healed in order to return to our former life but to live differently, breaking down divisions in society that exclude others because of their nationality, gender, religion or education.

Where do we place borders that cannot be crossed? Whom do we consider untouchable because they come from cultural or religious backgrounds that we fear or despise? 'Where are the nine?' asked Jesus. The nine were back where had come from, safely on the right side of the border, healed of their exterior problems but locked once again into their old worldview. Only one, through faith, became well in the broader sense of the word, walked away from prejudice and realised his freedom.

Peter's confession

Jesus went on with his disciples to the villages of Caesarea Philippi; and on the way he asked his disciples, 'Who do people say that I am?' And they answered him, 'John the Baptist; and others, Elijah; and still others, one of the prophets.' He asked them, 'But who do you say that I am?' Peter answered him, 'You are the Messiah.' And he sternly ordered them not to tell anyone about him.

MARK 8:27–30

Round about the midpoint of Jesus' ministry, and the midpoint of Mark's Gospel, Jesus arrives at Caesarea Philippi, a principally Gentile city about 25 miles north-east of the Sea of Galilee, said to be the birthplace of the Greek god Pan. Here, on the outskirts of a city that was littered with Syrian and Greek temples and overshadowed by the white marble home of Caesar-worship, Jesus asks his disciples about his own identity. 'Who do people say that I am?' he begins, and follows it up with another question: 'Who do you say that I am?'

There's a variety of reasons why we might ask others to give us their assessment of us: if we're trying to work out how effective we're being in a particular situation, for instance, we might ask a colleague for their observations. Here, though, I think, Jesus wasn't asking the question for his own benefit but because he wanted the disciples to distinguish between their personal convictions and popular opinion. He gave them a leading question, and then another leading question, until Peter came out with the right answer.

Mark is clever in the way he arranges this story. If you look back through chapter 8, you'll see that he begins with the miracle of feeding the 4000, after which the Pharisees ask Jesus for a sign to prove his identity. (I sometimes wonder where they were when Jesus fed 4000 people with a couple of packed lunches, but that's another story.) Shortly after that, Jesus gets frustrated with the disciples for missing the point yet again, and says to them, 'Do you have eyes, and fail to see?' (v. 18). Then he heals a blind man who, in physical terms, can't see at all, but the healing is gradual rather than instant: Jesus has to lay hands on him twice before his sight is fully restored. It takes a couple of attempts before he sees clearly. Then comes this little moment when, again, Jesus asks the disciples who they think he is. The theme that Mark has built throughout the chapter is about seeing—not only literally but metaphorically. The healing of the blind man is mirrored in the way the disciples begin to understand—at first getting a vague impression, until finally Peter realises what it's all about and exclaims, 'You are the Christ!'

Jesus, however, doesn't sigh with relief and say, 'Fantastic! At last we've broken through! Now for goodness' sake go and let everyone else know!' No, he actually orders them not to tell anyone else. Just as the disciples have had to work it out for themselves, so Mark wants his readers to have to engage in the same process—seeing a little more clearly as each chapter of the story unfolds.

Throughout this Lenten journey we have been circling round the question of seeing God clearly, recognising that our perception of God is, like that of the half-healed man, hazy and vague. Yet knowing that we can't see clearly is no help to us, and our own attempts to clarify our vision don't work. We can't see God clearly except through the revelation that Jesus himself brings us. Like the disciples, we need to follow him, watch how he operates, listen to his words, and just hang around in his company until one day the penny drops. All Peter did to get the revelation was to stick around with Jesus for a long time until gradually the fog cleared and he realised who Jesus really was.

I also think it's significant that Jesus asked his disciples to say out loud what they thought about him. There is something about articulating what you think you know that makes it real. That's one reason why students have to write essays and share ideas in seminars and supervisions. Reading and listening to lectures supplies them with plenty of information and ideas but the information doesn't gel or take root until they do something with it for themselves. The process of talking and writing and discussing is more than just a means of transferring facts into their minds. In the process, something happens to the material they're dealing with: it becomes real to them, it becomes part of them, and they can then do something with that knowledge.

The disciples began by simply reiterating what other people were saying: 'Jesus is John the Baptist, a prophet come back.' In the process of saying out loud what they had heard, the revelation came to them. The combination of prophecy and teaching, reading the scriptures and daily experience of walking with Jesus suddenly crystallised for Peter and at last he saw clearly.

That, I think, is one reason why Jesus told them not to tell anyone else. Why? Because there's no point in telling someone the answer to a question they haven't processed yet. We can't give someone else a shortcut to a revelation about Jesus. They have to see it for themselves.

What you see is what you get

Then he began to teach them that the Son of Man must undergo great suffering, and be rejected by the elders, the chief priests, and the scribes, and be killed, and after three days rise again. He said all this quite openly. And Peter took him aside and began to rebuke him. But turning and looking at his disciples, he rebuked Peter and said, 'Get behind me, Satan! For you are setting your mind not on divine things but on human things.'

MARK 8:31–33

I've always felt a bit sorry for poor old Peter here. Not five minutes earlier, he was the one—the only one—who managed to break through the clouds of confusion and see Jesus for who he was. And now Jesus gives him one of the sharpest rebukes we ever hear coming from his lips. What did Peter do to deserve that?

Peter had just seen and spoken the revelation that Jesus was the Messiah. Then, to hear Jesus telling them that he would suffer, be rejected and die was too much information to take in. How could this be possible? How could the Messiah die?

Perhaps, like any good friend would do, he was leaping to Jesus' defence. Perhaps he thought Jesus was having a rough day, feeling a bit down and tired and in need of some encouragement. Perhaps he was worried about the other disciples and their morale. Who knows what was going on in Peter's head?

Jesus was, I think, hearing echoes of the earlier conversation he'd had in the wilderness, confronting an invitation into the ways of darkness and death (Matthew 4:5–6). 'You don't need to die, Jesus,' says Peter, and perhaps Jesus sees again the glittering promise of Satan himself, the vision of angels bearing him up lest he strike his foot against a stone. We often imagine Jesus dealing with his temptations as a one-off in the wilderness and never again being troubled by the weaknesses of humanity that the rest of us have to confront. Yet Peter's words are, in fact, a reiteration of that earlier temptation.

The writer to the Hebrews says that Jesus was tested in every way as we are, yet without sin (4:15). One of the things we have to face about temptation is its repetitive nature. We don't get over temptations and find that they never bother us again. Whatever our Achilles heel might be—gossip, negativity, greed, pride, keeping a record of wrongs, anger or whatever—it's not something we deal with once and file away. We have to develop daily discipline to avoid being tripped up by our own weaknesses.

Mark tells us that Jesus spoke 'quite openly' about his own death. As we've already seen, Mark portrays Jesus as rather mysterious about his identity, and the disciples as slow to grasp what was really going on. But here at this point of revelation, it's as if the curtains are pulled back and Jesus is doing some straight talking, explaining to his disciples the reality of the situation.

There's also something interesting about the stage directions in this paragraph, which perhaps reveal something of the dynamics of the conversation. After Jesus has spoken openly to all the disciples, Peter takes Jesus on one side— out of earshot of the other disciples—to persuade him that his death is not necessary. Peter feels the need to have this conversation privately, but, before he replies to Peter, Jesus looks back at the other disciples. The others might not hear the conversation but the concerns of the whole group are still central to Jesus.

When people have a well-crafted public persona, it's interesting, and something of a privilege, to have the chance to meet them in private and continue a more personal conversation. It's one of the most impressive things, I think, to find that someone is not substantially different in private than they are in public. In the course of my work I have occasionally met people who preach a gospel of love, equality, forgiveness and grace, only to discover that behind the scenes they gossip and connive and control people. But I've also met some real saints—men and women who consistently live out what they say in public. Here, as Peter pulls Jesus to one side for a private conversation, he finds that Jesus isn't willing to say one thing in public but reveal a different, private self only to his close friends. Jesus looks back at the disciples and, even as he speaks in private, he maintains his integrity. What you see is what you get.

It's an important point, not just about the integrity of Jesus, but for understanding God as Trinity. Sometimes, when people speak of Jesus' death on the cross, they make it sound almost as if God the Father is angry and ready to punish sin, and only Jesus will persuade him to forgive our sins. But there is no God with a private agenda, hiding behind the public persona of Jesus. The Trinity is not divided; the reality is that God— Father, Son and Spirit—is all of a piece. What you see is what you get.

Take up your cross

[Jesus] called the crowd with his disciples, and said to them, 'If any want to become my followers, let them deny themselves and take up their cross and follow me. For those who want to save their life will lose it, and those who lose their life for my sake, and for the sake of the gospel, will save it. For what will it profit them to gain the whole world and forfeit their life? Indeed, what can they give in return for their life? Those who are ashamed of me and of my words in this adulterous and sinful generation, of them the Son of Man will also be ashamed when he comes in the glory of his Father with the holy angels.'

MARK 8:34–38

We've already considered the possibility that God's call is not always something that we don't want to do but might just as easily be something we're naturally drawn to, something that brings us joy and fulfilment. Moses discovered God's call when he followed a sight that intrigued him. Elsewhere in the Gospels, Jesus says that his yoke is easy and his burden is light (Matthew 11:30), but this passage from Mark 8 seems to contradict the idea of a light burden. The image of a yoke is related to work: it makes it possible and comfortable for an animal to carry a load, or, in the case of a double yoke, for two animals to work together as a team. But a cross goes far beyond that kind of burden. It's a punishing image, suggesting that if we follow Jesus we too may end up paying with our lives. How do we make sense of this? Must we simply revert to the idea that God is a hard taskmaster?

The first thing I notice in the story is that Jesus called both the crowd and his disciples. He's not speaking here only to those who have already been following him. This is a universal call, one that includes everyone. Perhaps it's a call to a fundamental decision over whether you want to follow Jesus: if you do, you need to know that there will be a cost involved. If you want to avoid difficulty, you shouldn't set out to follow him at all.

Nevertheless, as someone pointed out to me recently, we are called to carry our own cross and not someone else's. I remember, as a teenager, attending a church that had strong links with a mission station in Africa. Every few months, another missionary would make a trip home and would show us pictures and tell stories of what God was doing in Africa. They would tell us about the difficulties of life over there—the heat, the snakes, the food, the desert, the rural isolation— and it sounded to me like absolute torture. Then came the rub: they would say how none of these deprivations mattered compared to the knowledge that they were serving God. I remember sitting in that church so many Sundays in a state of conflict, wanting to say 'yes' to God, yet horrified at the prospect of the misery that seemed inevitable if I did.

Of course, the 'Africa' that horrified me as a teenager was an idea in my head. The dry, drab 'calling' I had been shown in a chilly little corner of England bore no relation to the reality— the brilliance, the colours, the vitality or the variety—of Africa itself. What I really needed to learn, though, was nothing to do with Africa itself, but that the call of God is strikingly different for each person. Certainly there are gospel imperatives that none of us can ignore: we must live in love and generosity and we must care for the poor; choosing to follow Christ will, at some level or other, cost us something. Despite that cost, though, God still doesn't call us to centre our lives in places where we are fundamentally ill at ease. We're called to find out where we fit best and then to follow that way, knowing that it will bring deep-seated challenge as well as joys.

Jesus adds a further bite to the challenge of following him with his statement that if we are ashamed of him now on earth, he will be ashamed of us in the future and other dimension that we refer to mysteriously as 'heaven'. Making sense of Jesus' teachings about heaven and his future coming in glory is hard enough just from the point of view of trying to understand what he meant in his own time. In the 21st century, separated from New Testament times by huge leaps in understanding of the cosmos, talk of heaven and future glory is even more shrouded in mystery than it was then.

For me, it makes little sense to try to be too prescriptive about what there is beyond the horizon: attempting any clear description of where or what heaven might be almost immediately results in saying things that can't possibly be true. The more important issue in Jesus' words is the idea of separation. I don't think he is threatening his disciples in a vengeful way, with a payback of denying them later if they deny him now. That would, at the least, be completely contradictory to the flow of his teachings. This is, after all, the same Jesus who not only demanded that justice should be limited to an eye for an eye and nothing more, but then called for forgiveness and an end to tit-for-tat retribution (Matthew 5:38–42).

By speaking of shame, Jesus shifts the argument from re- ward and punishment to relational closeness or separation. The concern here is not 'What do I have to do to get to heaven?' but 'How can I draw close to God?' Notice that Jesus doesn't threaten to exclude people but says that he will be ashamed of them. The point isn't about whether we get rewards or punishment; the point is that we can't live with two sets of values at the same time. If we want to live with the values of truth and justice and peace and love, we need to stand by them, whatever others may say. If it matters to us to believe in God, we need to be able to say so, even when everyone else disagrees. It's not about avoiding punishment; it's an issue of integrity, of holding ourself together as one piece. To believe in something and pretend otherwise will lead eventually to an internal division, and this is what lies behind the idea that shame could ultimately separate us from God.

To be? Or to do?

Six days later, Jesus took with him Peter and James and his brother John and led them up a high mountain, by themselves. And he was transfigured before them, and his face shone like the sun, and his clothes became dazzling white. Suddenly there appeared to them Moses and Elijah, talking with him. Then Peter said to Jesus, 'Lord, it is good for us to be here; if you wish, I will make three dwellings here, one for you, one for Moses, and one for Elijah.' While he was still speaking, suddenly a bright cloud overshadowed them, and from the cloud a voice said, 'This is my Son, the Beloved; with him I am well pleased; listen to him!' When the disciples heard this, they fell to the ground and were overcome by fear. But Jesus came and touched them, saying, 'Get up and do not be afraid.' And when they looked up, they saw no one except Jesus himself alone. As they were coming down the mountain, Jesus ordered them, 'Tell no one about the vision until after the Son of Man has been raised from the dead.'

MATTHEW 17:1–9

By recent tradition, the transfiguration is celebrated the week before Lent begins, but there's method in my madness in drawing it into our Lent readings: together with Peter's confession of faith, it is supremely a story about the confusion a popular and all-too-human concept of what God ought to be with the actual revelation of God in Jesus.

Quite often the Gospel stories begin with a seemingly incidental bit of narrative, in which Jesus leads his friends out into the desert or down to the sea or up a mountain—but sometimes the location has more significance than we would first suppose. As we have seen already, mountains are usually symbolic in the Bible: whenever an important revelation of God was given in the Old Testament, a mountain was highly likely to figure as the location. Here on top of this mountain Moses and Elijah, representing the Law and the Prophets, meet face to face with the Word of God incarnate. Only days before the transfiguration, Simon Peter, having known the human face of Jesus, had come out with his bold declaration of faith: 'You are the Messiah, the Son of the living God' (Matthew 16:16). Now, on the mountain top, Jesus confirms Peter's faith with this extraordinary revelation of divine glory. Jesus' face shone 'like the sun'—not like the moon, whose light is reflected and indirect, but like the sun, the full glory of God.

Faced with a revelation of God's glory, it is common for biblical figures to have a dramatic reaction: often they fall face down on the ground, either as a deliberate act of worship or simply in a dead faint. In the dazzling presence of Jesus in all his glory on the island of Patmos, John passed out, needing to be revived (Revelation 1:17), and here on this mountain, it seems that James and John may have done something similar. Their words and actions are not recorded, but certainly by the end of the story all three disciples were face down on the ground and shaking.

Peter's initial reaction was different, though. An activist by nature, his instant reaction to seeing the glory was not to sit down and listen, or to fall down and worship, but to jump up and do something. 'What do you want me to do, Lord?

Here, I could start building something right now—shelters for the three of you...' To Peter, it didn't come naturally to pause, listen, wait, think or worship. The presence of God made him want to act—to make things better, make the place suitable for the presence of God, change the world, change people's minds.

This wasn't a fault; it was Peter's personality. His impulsive nature and his big mouth got him into trouble sometimes, but they also gave him his greatest moments of glory: it was Peter, not John the mystic, who walked on the water; Peter who got to the beach breakfast first; Peter to whom Jesus entrusted the keys of the kingdom (Matthew 14:28–29; John 21:7–8; Matthew 16:19). Of course we need mystics and thinkers—the Church would be a shallow place without them—but nothing would ever get built if they were in charge of operations.

This passage highlights the contrast between Peter the activist and John the contemplative. We hear nothing of John in this story except that, along with James, he takes in the scene in awed silence. It's Peter who takes centre stage, talking too much and thinking of an action plan. Their reactions typify the way people react in situations where they feel overawed. From time to time I find myself at a college dining table with someone of truly outstanding intellect and achievements. My natural reaction would be to get completely tongue-tied and incapable of saying anything at all, let alone anything intelligent. Only part of my academic training was about learning to think: the rest was about learning how to unfreeze my brain under stress and stop myself clamming up and appearing completely stupid. But I quite often dine with a friend who is the complete opposite: he has the Simon Peter tendency. He talks volubly and articulately about a great many topics but occasionally, like Simon Peter, he can't stop talking even when he's run out of things to say. Our personalities are different, but what my friend and I have in common is that we've both found ourselves overwhelmed in the presence of greatness.

I love the gentleness of God's response to Peter's blathering. He doesn't say 'yes' or 'no' to the over-enthusiastic suggestion of building tents; instead he simply says, 'This is my Son—listen to him.' We have no way of reconstructing the tone of voice that God might have used but I imagine God smiling through the cloud, amused by and deeply affectionate towards Peter, as I am when my own son's youthful attempts at life slightly misfire.

When we pray, we need to forget about ourselves and our reactions and just listen. If you're an activist, you may well be destined to shoulder responsibility and build the kingdom of God, but before you do that, you need to learn that in the presence of God you need to stop jumping, stop talking, stop planning, and listen. If you're a contemplative and your brain freezes up in the presence of glory, you can learn to unfreeze it. You won't necessarily need to say anything—your job is not to be wise or clever in the presence of God—but you need a clear, calm head so that you too can listen.

Questions for reflection

- Does the way our community celebrates Mothering Sunday draw the community together as Mother Church or does it divide people? Do we dare flout the culture and do something different?
- Do I carry my own cross? Or do I try to carry someone else's?
- Do I tend to be an activist or a contemplative? What do I need to learn about listening to God?

Changing your mind

It's not fair

[Jesus] entered a certain village, where a woman named Martha welcomed him into her home. She had a sister named Mary, who sat at the Lord's feet and listened to what he was saying. But Martha was distracted by her many tasks; so she came to him and asked, 'Lord, do you not care that my sister has left me to do all the work by myself? Tell her then to help me.' But the Lord answered her, 'Martha, Martha, you are worried and distracted by many things; there is need of only one thing. Mary has chosen the better part, which will not be taken away from her.'

LUKE 10:38–42

It's always risky to apply any kind of psychological theory to historical characters. We can observe patterns in their stories and speculate about motivations and agendas, but any post-humous diagnosis of behaviour is unreliable, especially when it's based on small fragments of information. To read our modern-day psychological struggles into the Gospel characters is more speculative than historical. This goes even for Jesus himself, about whom we often feel we have a much clearer picture than we really do.

Nevertheless, as with any poetry or literature, the biblical accounts come to us not merely as a series of historical facts but as portraits through which we can see what it means to be human. Even when historical figures are sketchily drawn, it is a legitimate exercise to retell their story with a degree of speculation as to the interpretation of events. Even if such retellings elaborate on historical fact, they have their value as a means of extending our understanding of human nature and, in the case of the Gospels, absorbing some truth about ourselves in the light of Jesus.

We have only a few short stories about Lazarus and his sisters, Mary and Martha, who lived at Bethany near Jerusalem. Their interaction with Jesus suggests a close friendship rather than the moderated politeness of a formal relationship, and they are not idealised to us as perfect saints. Here and there we catch glimpses of raw emotion, such as in this family argument   •
that erupted when Mary sat at Jesus' feet listening to his stories while Martha did all the housework.

Some years ago, I visited Egypt in the course of my work, to speak and sing at Cairo Cathedral and then to travel south. My guide and interpreter for the trip was Hapi, a student from southern Egypt who was studying in the United States and was home on vacation. Hapi and I, with a couple of friends, were invited to visit some local people in their homes, and once we left the city for the rural areas further south, the cultural differences became more obvious. Whenever we visited a home, we were given a warm welcome by the men of the house and invited into the living room to talk. There we were waited on with food and drink by the wives and daughters of the household, to whom we were only briefly and distantly introduced. Apart from the times when they brought us tea and food, I was the only woman in the room. I caught sight of them peeping through the curtains from the kitchen, listening to the conversation. Hapi told me that they wouldn't come in to talk and I shouldn't go to talk to them in the kitchen, either, as I was a guest.

When Mary left the kitchen to sit at Jesus' feet, I wonder

what it was, exactly, that ruffled Martha's feathers. I would guess it was not just the kind of annoyance we feel with a housemate who leaves their unwashed dishes in the sink but the kind of frustration that can erupt when boundaries are crossed, when the status quo is upset, when someone ceases to act within their usual role.

Was Martha disturbed that Mary was breaking out of the accepted role for a woman, and wishing she would return to help in the kitchen? Was she angry at herself for not daring to abandon the kitchen and sit at Jesus' feet? Or was she angry with Jesus for upsetting the natural order of things, including a woman in a type of conversation usually reserved for men? It's interesting that rather than calling Mary back to the kitchen, Martha addressed her complaint to Jesus, leaving an ambiguity in her complaint: perhaps she was less annoyed about having been left to do the work alone and more concerned that Jesus was challenging the accepted role of women. Perhaps she was unnerved that friendship with Jesus opened up this radical possibility; perhaps she felt it to be more threatening than liberating.

The Gospels are packed full of stories and sayings and parables that invert the reader's expectations, turning convention upside down. We, too, have conventions and traditions with which we are comfortable, and the gospel equally stands as a call to turn them upside down. Whether this call appears to us as a promise or a threat will depend upon how much we need our conventions to make us feel safe and happy. For those who find church traditions frustrating, an invitation to turn them upside down may seem like a welcome promise. Yet the gospel is thorough: it does not favour one personality or culture over another. God's call will radically transform our lives whoever we are, and no matter what sort of church or spiritual tradition we belong to.

Sacred irreverence

When Jesus arrived, he found that Lazarus had already been in the tomb for four days. Now Bethany was near Jerusalem, some two miles away, and many of the Jews had come to Martha and Mary to console them about their brother. When Martha heard that Jesus was coming, she went and met him, while Mary stayed at home. Martha said to Jesus, 'Lord, if you had been here, my brother would not have died. But even now I know that God will give you whatever you ask of him.' Jesus said to her, 'Your brother will rise again.' Martha said to him, 'I know that he will rise again in the resurrection on the last day.' Jesus said to her, 'I am the resurrection and the life. Those who believe in me, even though they die, will live, and everyone who lives and believes in me will never die. Do you believe this?' She said to him, 'Yes, Lord, I believe that you are the Messiah, the Son of God, the one coming into the world.' …

He said, 'Where have you laid him?' They said to him, 'Lord, come and see.' Jesus began to weep. So the Jews said, 'See how he loved him!' But some of them said, 'Could not he who opened the eyes of the blind man have kept this man from dying?'

Then Jesus, again greatly disturbed, came to the tomb. It was a cave, and a stone was lying against it. Jesus said, 'Take away the stone.' Martha, the sister of the dead man, said to him, 'Lord, already there is a stench because he has been dead for four days.' Jesus said to her, 'Did I not tell you that if you believed, you would see the glory of God?' So they took away the stone. And Jesus looked upwards and said, 'Father, I thank you for having heard me. I knew that you always hear me, but I have said this for the sake of the crowd standing here, so that they may believe that you sent me.' When he had said this, he cried with a loud voice, 'Lazarus, come out!' The dead man came out, his hands and feet bound with strips of cloth, and his face wrapped in a cloth. Jesus said to them, 'Unbind him, and let him go.'

JOHN 11:17–27, 34–44

Yesterday we saw Martha complaining to Jesus when Mary left the kitchen to sit in the living room, listening to him. Now, as Jesus arrives at Bethany four days after Lazarus has died, we find Martha once again remonstrating with Jesus. 'If you had been here,' she says, 'Lazarus wouldn't have died.' Her words might have sounded angry, born of a feeling that Jesus had let them down and should have come sooner, or they could have been more like the unchecked words that spill out in moments of extreme distress or grief—the feeling of 'if only'.

If Jesus were a theologian, I guess he might have weighed in with a good theodicy—a theory as to why God allows evil—but he didn't take any opportunity to teach them or offer any justification of his actions. Instead he did two things that were completely unexpected.

The first thing he did was to weep. This seems puzzling: why did he cry if he knew he was about to raise Lazarus from the dead? Three possibilities occur to me. One is that he felt torn. If he knew (which we never will know this side of the grave) that Lazarus truly was in a better place, then bringing him back would have been something of a mixed blessing.

Another possibility is that Jesus' tears stemmed from frustration and sadness and compassion for a broken world that needed far more than one man—even a God-man—could give. He couldn't be everywhere at once; he couldn't be healing the sick and feeding the hungry and by his friend's side all at the same time. A third possibility is that Jesus recognised the fact that he was living on the edge of danger and his own death was imminent. Was he weeping in anticipation of the grief and pain of his own death a few days later?

After he wept, the second thing Jesus did was to order the stone to be rolled away—again, in something of a prophetic foreshadowing of his own resurrection. The tomb was opened and then Lazarus appeared, wrapped in a shroud, as his body came back to life.

By focusing on the miracle of a resurrection, we might miss the fact that there is something totally irreverent about this scene. There would have been a terrible smell of rotting flesh, the retching of people standing nearby, Jesus wet-faced and blotchy from weeping. None of this fits with our respectable, tidied-up ideas about God. Of course we like him to work miracles, but we want him to be clean, in control and smelling good, like a movie hero. However much we say that he was fully human, when it comes to the dirt, grime and indignity of all those things we like to keep private, we perhaps prefer Jesus to be a little transcendent. Wouldn't it be disrespectful otherwise? Are we really allowed to contemplate a Jesus with real tears and a runny nose? Yet resurrections, for all that they must be magnificent, are surely no more clean or dignified than births.

The principle of resurrection can touch us at different levels. It can be a matter of finding a new lease of life when things have become dead and dull, of seeing a far wider perspective when our vision of life's possibilities has become stunted. For

Lazarus, resurrection was literal and physical: he rose out of his grave, just as Jesus would do a few days later. What about the people who witnessed it, though? I wonder whether they discovered a resurrection of their own—whether they rose above the mundane yet equally imprisoning spiritual and emotional deadness that can haunt everyday life. Perhaps Martha discovered that the habit of blaming God meant living in some sense under the shadow of death. Perhaps others realised that life without hope, obsessed with themselves, with no capacity to give or share or celebrate, was a kind of living death. Sometimes we continue for years in shades of grey until a catastrophe, a startling event, jolts us out of our rut and makes us grasp the gift of life with both hands.

Such resurrections, even though they are not physical, may be just as messy and undignified as that of Lazarus. We may have to put up with some unpalatable disorder in the process of leaving grey behind for a life in full colour. Sometimes we spend years enduring jobs, churches, schools or marriages that are crushing our spirits before we find the courage to change our lives. Radical change is hard work, and will happen only if we take the risk that tears will be shed and our dignity shattered. We have to let go of the control and order that were so important to Martha. We don't get resurrection if we insist on Jesus obeying our timetable or being as dignified as we would like him to be.

Australian poet Noel Rowe calls this abandonment of dignity a 'sacred irreverence':

… a gift to those found free
in the spirit. Even Zaccheus found it in himself, up a tree,
and Lazarus, sauntering around in his shroud.[7]

To discover this freedom of spirit, we have to allow ourselves to be fully, failingly human, and let go of our ideas of respectability and religious rules. They are rules that God himself will surely refuse to obey, so we should not let them set limits on us, either.

Fast and slow

That same day Jesus went out of the house and sat beside the lake. Such great crowds gathered around him that he got into a boat and sat there, while the whole crowd stood on the beach. And he told them many things in parables, saying: 'Listen! A sower went out to sow. And as he sowed, some seeds fell on the path, and the birds came and ate them up. Other seeds fell on rocky ground, where they did not have much soil, and they sprang up quickly, since they had no depth of soil. But when the sun rose, they were scorched; and since they had no root, they withered away. Other seeds fell among thorns, and the thorns grew up and choked them. Other seeds fell on good soil and brought forth grain, some a hundredfold, some sixty, some thirty. Let anyone with ears listen!'

MATTHEW 13:1–9

One of the things I love to do when I'm reading the Bible is to stop for a moment and dwell on the little phrases that connect the stories together. We've just read the parable of the sower, and this famous story can immediately set your mind buzzing with analogies. What did Jesus mean by the seeds? What were the different kinds of soil? Was he talking about mission or spirituality?

Before we think about the sower, however, let's go right

back to the first sentence. What do you see? Jesus, we are told, went out and sat on the beach. Pause for a moment and picture the scene. What does it feel like to sit on the beach? You might think of relaxing on a hot summer's day with lapping waves and the sounds of children playing in the distance. Or you might think of a walk along a deserted beach in winter, a stiff wind blowing away the cobwebs, before you sit down in the shelter of a large sand dune to watch the waves crashing.

The Gospels are littered with phrases that mention Jesus going out on his own to pray—down to the sea, up a mountain, or anywhere he could be alone. Mark says that Jesus got up early, while it was still dark, to go to a solitary place where he prayed (1:35); Luke says he often withdrew to lonely places and prayed (5:16). Here, though, it doesn't say that Jesus went down to the lake to pray; it simply says that he went and sat.

A couple of years ago, a friend of mine came to stay in my house while carrying out a research project. One evening, I was cooking dinner when the phone rang. While I was answering it, I also nipped upstairs to see if my son was out of the bath yet, and then the doorbell rang, and after I'd answered it the phone rang again. I got back to the kitchen to resume cooking, at which point my friend, who had taken over preparing dinner, put a glass of wine in my hand, pointed to the chair in the corner of the kitchen and said with a smile, 'Sit down! Now! Honestly, don't you ever just sit and do nothing?'

I was surprised to find how hard it was to stay sitting down for more than a few minutes while someone else took the strain. It took a good ten minutes to wind down and become properly still.

There are times when the flow of life seems to pull us into more and more activity, until we forget how to stop and be still. I used to be better at it, I think, before I began the juggling act of bringing up a child and holding down a job, but the tendency to let life become frenetic is not the sole preserve of mothers; it gets all sorts of people for all sorts of reasons.

Our culture likes speed: we like things to go faster and smoother and more efficiently. Of course, in some areas of life, speed is highly desirable. Clearing bureaucratic hurdles at speed is good; having a computer that runs quickly and efficiently is good; the post arriving on time is good. There are other ways in which speed is not so good for us, though—fast food, eating too fast, driving too fast, never having the time to pause and take stock or to look into someone's eyes and really listen to what they are saying. Author Carl Honoré, in his book *In Praise of Slow*, calls this the cult of speed: not just speeding up what needs to go faster, but a kind of winding up of the whole of life until it's like a centrifuge that pins us to its revolutions.[8]

Even our spirituality can be subject to this tendency towards speed and drivenness. Jesus went to sit by the sea and get the space he needed but he soon found himself besieged by the crowds, who wanted more of him. So from his moment of stillness he pitched out in a boat and began to tell them his stories.

He told them about a farmer who walked about throwing seeds on to his land. The seeds went everywhere and, no doubt, he knew that some of them would come to nothing, because if you're going to grow things, some seeds are always wasted. Then there were seeds that were eaten up by the birds in no time, and others that started well but grew too fast and couldn't mature for lack of depth.

The ones that did grow, though, were the ones that vanished for a while—sank a bit deeper into good soil. They didn't sprout so quickly, but this was good, because they were putting down roots first. And when they eventually came up, they didn't grow quickly at all. They grew at the proper speed, developing strong stems and good fat seed heads.

Spirituality that bears fruit is not a fast-food business. We can try to make the kingdom of heaven more efficient if we want to; we can try to maximise effort and produce more fruit per hour of work. But in the end, like growing wheat, real spiritual growth has an optimum speed, and accelerating the growth and maximising the harvest will be about as much good for the soul as fast food is for the body. Some things just take time.

I'm off to sit on the beach for a while now. See you tomorrow.

The good Samaritan

A lawyer stood up to test Jesus. 'Teacher,' he said, 'what must I do to inherit eternal life?' He said to him, 'What is written in the law? What do you read there?' He answered, 'You shall love the Lord your God with all your heart, and with all your soul, and with all your strength, and with all your mind; and your neighbour as yourself.' And he said to him, 'You have given the right answer; do this, and you will live.'

But wanting to justify himself, he asked Jesus, 'And who is my neighbour?' Jesus replied, 'A man was going down from Jerusalem to Jericho, and fell into the hands of robbers, who stripped him, beat him, and went away, leaving him half dead. Now by chance a priest was going down that road; and when he saw him, he passed by on the other side. So likewise a Levite, when he came to the place and saw him, passed by on the other side. But a Samaritan while travelling came near him; and when he saw him, he was moved with pity. He went to him and bandaged his wounds, having poured oil and wine on them. Then he put him on his own animal, brought him to an inn, and took care of him. The next day he took out two denarii, gave them to the innkeeper, and said, "Take care of him; and when I come back, I will repay you whatever more you spend." Which of these three, do you think, was a neighbour to the man who fell into the hands of the robbers?' He said, 'The one who showed him mercy.' Jesus said to him, 'Go and do likewise.'

LUKE 10:25–37

Luke is one of the best storytellers in the Bible. His Gospel is full of little thumbnail sketches of moments in people's lives when they met Jesus and what happened next. It's Luke who gives us the prodigal son, Zacchaeus climbing the sycamore tree, and Martha and Mary fighting over the housework. But the trouble with looking at old favourites like the good Samaritan is that we tend to pay less attention because we think we already know the story.

It's well documented that Jews absolutely despised Samaritans and would travel miles out of their way simply to avoid setting foot inside Samaria. In fact, only a few paragraphs earlier in Luke's Gospel, Jesus himself had been sent packing from a Samaritan village (9:52–53). The good Samaritan, though, understood that, whatever the rest of the world thought, the Jew dying by the roadside was simply a fellow human being. The meaning of the story is clear: don't be bound by ethnic and religious bigotry; instead, be like the Samaritan and be led by your humanity.

I wonder, though, whether the lesson might be brought home in a different way if we consider the story from another point of view than that of the good Samaritan. What happens to the story if you imagine that you are the Jew dying by the roadside?

It's easy to think that when you're in a bad way, any help would be better than none, but the truth is that, even when people are desperately ill, they still have feelings. A few years ago, I went to visit a friend of mine in hospital. He'd had peritonitis but it had initially been misdiagnosed and, by the time his operation was carried out, it was touch and go whether he would recover. He was in his 20s and had a wife and two small boys, so the tragedy would have been multiplied if he hadn't made it. Oddly, though, what really upset him was not that he'd nearly died but that he'd had to endure so many indignities in hospital—being dressed and washed and brought bedpans by strangers. Being helped by people we don't know is not only humiliating; it can also be frightening. We have a built-in reserve about those who don't look or act like us, because we don't know what to expect from them.

A long time ago, when I lived in London, I was coming home one afternoon when there was a delay on the Underground. My train was packed to the gills with rush-hour commuters, it was hot and airless, and we had been stuck in the tunnel for quite some time. Eventually the train began to move again but, by the time we were pulling into Victoria Station, I was feeling really ill and pretty sure I was going to faint. I got off the train and walked unsteadily across the platform, looking for help. Coming towards me was a smart, well-dressed woman with a kind face. Surely she would help? As she drew level with me, I said, 'Help me, please, I'm going to faint', but she gave me a funny look and walked away quickly.

Right behind her was a man in a business suit, carrying a briefcase, and I asked him to help, but he mumbled an apology and hurried off down the platform. They had appeared to me like pillars of society but they clearly didn't want some sick person making them late for their business meetings.

The next thing that happened was that I did faint, right there on the platform. When I came round, I was alarmed to find myself looking up at the strangely decorated faces of six or seven people who had gathered round me. One man had tattoos all over his face, neck and arms, and one girl had a huge shock of bright red dreadlocks. The girls wore pale make-up and thick black eyeliner and extraordinary hairstyles; they all wore huge dangerous-looking boots, and pretty much every visible body part was pierced several times over. They were leaning over me and several of them were reaching out their hands towards me.

As well as feeling ill, I now also felt conspicuously conservative and very vulnerable. These people were not like me, not from my culture, and I was afraid of them. But as the ringing in my ears began to stop, I realised that one of the women was talking to me very gently, asking if I knew my name, if I knew where I was, telling me that the ambulance was coming, that she had my belongings safe, that I need not worry. They looked after me, came with me to the hospital and later took me home. I never saw them again.

Whenever we come across someone who is clearly very different from us, where we find an invisible cultural barrier between us and them, we face the same challenge as the dying Jew. Are we going to let this alien, perhaps even offensive person give us a fresh possibility of life, or are we going to refuse their help and wait for someone we like better? It's sobering to remember that had the Jew in the story refused the Samaritan's aid, he might well have been dead by the time the next offer of help came along. Life, if we let it, will throw us together with people who are not like us—different in background and culture, interests and occupations, politics and religion, accent and income. God calls us not only to be good to others across such cultural boundaries but also to be vulnerable to them and allow them be good to us, so that through them we catch a glimpse of God's love.

Of course we can learn from the radical love of the Samaritan, but let's also learn something from the dying Jew and become humble enough to receive help, care, insight and friendship from all kinds of people, whether or not, superficially speaking, they are 'our kind of people'.

The man who had everything...

A certain ruler asked him, 'Good Teacher, what must I do to inherit eternal life?' Jesus said to him, 'Why do you call me good? No one is good but God alone. You know the commandments: "You shall not commit adultery; You shall not murder; You shall not steal; You shall not bear false witness; Honour your father and mother."' He replied, 'I have kept all these since my youth.' When Jesus heard this, he said to him, 'There is still one thing lacking. Sell all that you own and distribute the money to the poor, and you will have treasure in heaven; then come, follow me.' But when he heard this, he became sad; for he was very rich. Jesus looked at him and said, 'How hard it is for those who have wealth to enter the kingdom of God! Indeed, it is easier for a camel to go through the eye of a needle than for someone who is rich to enter the kingdom of God.'

Those who heard it said, 'Then who can be saved?' He replied, 'What is impossible for mortals is possible for God.' Then Peter said, 'Look, we have left our homes and followed you.' And he said to them, 'Truly I tell you, there is no one who has left house or wife or brothers or parents or children, for the sake of the kingdom of God, who will not get back very much more in this age, and in the age to come eternal life.'

LUKE 18:18–30

This story is usually entitled 'The rich young ruler'—and rich he certainly was, according to Luke, who uses the Greek words *plousios sphodra*, meaning 'abundantly wealthy'. Although Luke doesn't mention his age, Matthew's parallel account says that he was a young man (19:20), and he was a ruler, someone with administrative responsibility, in this context most probably a religious leader in the synagogue or the Sanhedrin.

All the Gospel writers place this story towards the end of Jesus' ministry, and Mark's version tells us that it was just as Jesus was about to leave town that the man ran up to him (10:17). I wonder, if the young ruler was so influential, why he waited until Jesus was just about to leave before he stopped him with this burning question. Maybe he had been sceptical at first, and watched from the sidelines, unconvinced that this itinerant preacher could have anything to offer a sophisticated man like him. Whatever the reason, at the very last minute he ran to Jesus to speak with him personally and ask him how to inherit eternal life.

The lawyer in yesterday's reading had asked Jesus exactly the same question, but he seemed more interested in winning an argument than getting a genuine answer to his question (Luke 10:25–29). The rich young ruler seems to be sincere. Perhaps he perceived a fundamental difference between himself and Jesus and saw that, despite being a religious leader with an impeccable record, he still had little grasp on what life was all about. Seeing a depth of vitality in Jesus, he wanted to know what the missing ingredient was. His question, 'How do I inherit eternal life?' seems to go way beyond issues of doctrine, asking at a fundamental level what is the meaning and purpose of life.

The young ruler begins by addressing Jesus respectfully and politely. 'Good teacher,' he begins—but Jesus brushes this away, saying that only God is good. Jesus is somewhat brusque in a number of places in the Gospels: for instance, he refused to answer his family's call on his time (Matthew 12:46–50), and was actually offensive to a woman from Syrophoenicia (Mark 7:25–30), calling her a dog. Why was he so short with the rich young ruler? It could well be that he was cutting straight through the social niceties to demonstrate that he was unimpressed by the games of social politics. Jesus could have exchanged pleasantries but what this man really needed was a straight answer to his question, so Jesus dismissed the formal address and got straight to the point.

What becomes immediately apparent from the brief conversation is that the ruler was quintessentially the Man Who Had Everything—immense wealth, good social standing, influence in society and a moral character beyond reproach. He really did have it all, and yet, somewhere in the core of his being, he knew there was something missing. Jesus hit the nail on the head: 'There is still one thing lacking,' he said.

What the man lacked was not another material possession, achievement or aspect of moral development but the ability to make things flow in the other direction—to give rather than to draw things to himself. All that he had achieved, all he had accrued, all the respect and good standing he had attained, all these were worth nothing if this most important piece of the jigsaw was not in place.

The solution, Jesus told him, was simple: reverse the flow. The meaning of life is the one thing money can't buy; it comes to you when you start giving, so sell your possessions and give to the poor. It was in this simple commandment that the source of the problem emerged. It wasn't the wealth in itself; it was the fact that the man was owned by his possessions, not the other way round. When it came to the crunch, he couldn't part with them, even though they stood in the way of his receiving what he needed most of all.

Just in case we were going to make the mistake of thinking that this particular challenge applies only to very wealthy people, the point is then given an extra twist in Jesus' conversation with Peter. No sooner has the rich man found himself unable to part with his great wealth than Peter points out that he and the other disciples, men of moderate means, have already left their homes and livelihoods to follow Jesus. Yet Jesus seems singularly unimpressed with that argument, too. 'So what?' he seems to shrug. 'You'll get back whatever is really important.'

The issue is not about how much wealth or power we have, but how much mental space it occupies. A person who has very little, or has given things up to follow Jesus, can be more preoccupied with anxiety or resentment about money than someone who owns a lot but for whom it is merely a tool for life. Jesus told the rich young ruler to give away his possessions because he needed to be freed from their hold over him, but in the next breath Jesus dismissed any kind of self-congratulation on the part of those who really had given up their livelihoods to follow him. His words to Peter emphasise that the point is not whether we have money or not; it's whether thinking about it and managing it begins to take over space in our soul that it shouldn't occupy. Again, it's about the flow: do we draw possessions and power in to ourselves, or do we give back to the society we live in? Charitable works and self-sacrifice, like wealth, can be a cork in the bottle of human relationships if they too become self-serving.

Born again

Now there was a Pharisee named Nicodemus, a leader of the Jews. He came to Jesus by night and said to him, 'Rabbi, we know that you are a teacher who has come from God; for no one can do these signs that you do apart from the presence of God.' Jesus answered him, 'Very truly, I tell you, no one can see the kingdom of God without being born from above.' Nicodemus said to him, 'How can anyone be born after having grown old? Can one enter a second time into the mother's womb and be born?' Jesus answered, 'Very truly, I tell you, no one can enter the kingdom of God without being born of water and Spirit. What is born of the flesh is flesh, and what is born of the Spirit is spirit. Do not be astonished that I said to you, "You must be born from above." The wind blows where it chooses, and you hear the sound of it, but you do not know where it comes from or where it goes. So it is with everyone who is born of the Spirit.'

JOHN 3:1–8

Why did Nicodemus come to Jesus by night? What's the significance of this night-time assignation? Some say that he came under the cover of darkness because he didn't want his fellow Pharisees to know he was meeting Jesus, that he only wanted to acknowledge Jesus privately—and the lesson is that we can't follow Jesus unless we do so openly and publicly. A kinder reading might point out that Nicodemus came to Jesus, despite his fear, the only way he knew how. In fact, there are scholars who have put forward the idea that John's Gospel was written originally to strengthen and encourage a group of Christians who were struggling with the public confession of their faith for fear of being ostracised or persecuted.

It's equally possible, though, that John added the detail about the night simply to make a point about spiritual enlightenment. John uses symbolic oppositions throughout his Gospel—light and darkness, life and death, heaven and earth. Taken metaphorically, the story tells us that Nicodemus was spiritually in the dark until he came to the light of Christ.

When Nicodemus heard that he must be born again, he was baffled as to what Jesus meant. Centuries later, 'born again' has acquired another set of difficulties of interpretation. These two words have become something of a grenade in spiritual language by being strongly associated with a particular cultural expression of Christianity.

I remember, as a teenager, taking part in a street mission with my local church. I was teamed up with someone who was considered to be an experienced evangelist, and we fell into conversation with someone who had stopped to watch our street theatre. 'I suppose you're one of those "born again" enthusiasts, then?' he asked, with a look of scorn, and the comments that followed made it clear that his idea of God had been coloured by an experience of an overbearing, intellectually shallow form of Christianity.

'No, I wouldn't say that at all,' I replied, and began to suggest that there might be more to Christianity than he had seen thus far. Unfortunately, the senior evangelist immediately weighed in and began to tear strips off me for (as he saw it) denying my faith. The result was a complete impasse. The man who had stopped to talk only knew one narrow meaning of 'born again' and was keen to avoid having anything to do with it; the evangelist was certain about its meaning and couldn't depart from the language he was used to; I stood between them, attempting to cross a communication barrier but not succeeding. Nobody seemed to be meeting Jesus that afternoon.

We can fall into a double trap when we tread around the complexities of language and meaning. On the one hand, unless we question and critique the words we use and the ideas they convey, we may miss much of their meaning. On the other hand, if we spend too much time focused on what things are not, we do the spiritual equivalent of walking down the street trying to avoid stepping on the cracks. We may end up being perfectly precise about what we mean but all we ever see is the pavement, not the big blue sky.

The desire to distance ourselves from one expression of Christianity or another shouldn't keep us from grasping the words of Jesus: we must be born, not only physically but spiritually as well. It isn't necessarily the case that being 'born again' refers to a unique moment of conversion, though. What's important about birth is not identifying the exact moment that it happens, but recognising that a baby is alive. It's the same with spiritual birth: we don't need to remember the moment, but we do need to know we're alive.

From a Christian point of view, spiritual life involves both an infilling of the Holy Spirit and our own spirits being brought to life within us. We need to come to Jesus not just once, but whenever the darkness falls upon our souls and threatens to drain the life from us.

Loving and giving

Nicodemus said to [Jesus], 'How can these things be?' Jesus answered him, 'Are you a teacher of Israel, and yet you do not understand these things? Very truly, I tell you, we speak of what we know and testify to what we have seen; yet you do not receive our testimony. If I have told you about earthly things and you do not believe, how can you believe if I tell you about heavenly things? No one has ascended into heaven except the one who descended from heaven, the Son of Man. And just as Moses lifted up the serpent in the wilderness, so must the Son of Man be lifted up, that whoever believes in him may have eternal life.

'For God so loved the world that he gave his only Son, so that everyone who believes in him may not perish but may have eternal life. Indeed, God did not send the Son into the world to condemn the world, but in order that the world might be saved through him. Those who believe in him are not condemned; but those who do not believe are condemned already, because they have not believed in the name of the only Son of God. And this is the judgment, that the light has come into the world, and people loved darkness rather than light because their deeds were evil. For all who do evil hate the light and do not come to the light, so that their deeds may not be exposed. But those who do what is true come to the light, so that it may be clearly seen that their deeds have been done in God.'

JOHN 3:9–21

On a recent trip to the United States, I saw several people wearing a T-shirt of the same design. A plain-coloured shirt had emblazoned across the front, in large letters, just one word and three numbers: 'John 3:16'. This single verse from John's Gospel is the most-quoted verse from the entire Bible, although on this side of the Atlantic, whenever it's posted on roadside billboards, church noticeboards or in the London Underground, the text itself is invariably quoted along with the reference—a stark reminder that in the USA a residual knowledge of the Bible can be assumed to a much greater degree than it can in the UK. John 3:16 is considered by many to be the most eloquent summary of the gospel: 'For God so loved the world that he gave his only Son, so that everyone who believes in him may not perish but may have eternal life.'

The regularity with which this verse is quoted and, perhaps, the perception of it as a neat gospel formula can serve to reduce its impact through overfamiliarity. Perhaps, for the Christian, it seems like an entry-level text—a step in the manual of faith that, once taken, cannot be taken again. But the movement of the verse reveals one of the most important theological statements of all—that because God loves, he gives himself. There is a matching movement in Philippians 2:5–8, which tells us that Jesus emptied himself of the likeness of God. In other words, for God to give his only begotten Son involved a supreme act of self-emptying, of self-giving. God did not just give us a gift, something apart from himself that he could hand over—a set of laws, for instance. Nor even did he 'give' his Son in the sense that Jesus was separate from him. God and his Son are inseparable, and so, in giving us his Son, God gave us himself.

Karl Barth, one of the greatest and most prolific theologians of the 20th century, wrote volume after volume of his major work, *Church Dogmatics*. I was told as a student that it ran, in total, to about six million words. Someone once asked Barth in an interview whether he could sum up the heart of his theology. The interviewer must have been waiting with bated breath for some great nugget of truth as Barth sat thoughtfully for a few moments. Eventually he smiled and said, 'Jesus loves me, this I know, for the Bible tells me so.'

In the end, although it may require thousands of words and innumerable acts of kindness to make sense of it, the truth is simple: God is love and, because he is love, he gives himself. Love cannot but give itself. You can't love someone and withhold yourself: the two things are contrary.

Taken out of context, John 3:16 could seem to suggest that if we do not believe, we are therefore condemned, but the completion of the saying in the following two verses denies this idea. First, John affirms that 'God did not send his Son into the world to condemn the world, but in order that the world might be saved through him'. John makes it clear that he sees the salvation of the world as God's intent from the outset. The spotlight is placed not on the condemnation of the world but on God's grace and salvation.

John 3:16 calls for a response, then, not out of the fear of being condemned but because God offers us an invitation into life in all its fullness. We can condemn ourselves if we wish but that condemnation is not born in the heart of God. He is not out to trick us; he is love, and love never withholds itself. He is the God of light, not darkness; the God of life, not death.

Questions for reflection

- Do I ever try to accelerate my spiritual growth or the growth of other people? What does it mean to grow at the right pace?
- Do we need to be prepared to suffer a little indignity or accept a degree of irreverence in what we expect of God, in order to discover true freedom?
- Does wealth—either having it or not having it—occupy any more of my mental space than it should?
- Are there people (such as individuals, ethnic groups or religious groups) from whom we think it would be impossible to learn anything about God?
- Do I believe that I am completely forgiven and loved, without condemnation? Am I able to forgive others in the same way?

HOLY WEEK

'The end of all our exploring…'

T.S. ELIOT, 'LITTLE GIDDING', *FOUR QUARTETS*, 1942

A king on a donkey

When they were approaching Jerusalem, at Bethphage and Bethany, near the Mount of Olives, [Jesus] sent two of his disciples and said to them, 'Go into the village ahead of you, and immediately as you enter it, you will find tied there a colt that has never been ridden; untie it and bring it. If anyone says to you, "Why are you doing this?" just say this, "The Lord needs it and will send it back here immediately."' They went away and found a colt tied near a door, outside in the street. As they were untying it, some of the bystanders said to them, 'What are you doing, untying the colt?' They told them what Jesus had said; and they allowed them to take it. Then they brought the colt to Jesus and threw their cloaks on it; and he sat on it. Many people spread their cloaks on the road, and others spread leafy branches that they had cut in the fields. Then those who went ahead and those who followed were shouting, 'Hosanna! Blessed is the one who comes in the name of the Lord! Blessed is the coming kingdom of our ancestor David! Hosanna in the highest heaven!'

Then he entered Jerusalem and went into the temple; and when he had looked around at everything, as it was already late, he went out to Bethany with the twelve.

MARK 11:1–11

It's often assumed that the 'triumphal entry' was a way of declaring Jesus as the Messiah, announcing that the kingdom of God, which he had proclaimed for so long, at last had a king. It's unlikely, though, that the bystanders understood it as anything so blatant. For a start, we know that the Roman authorities were on edge about any potential uprising, and a public display with a clear messianic claim would have had Jesus arrested within the hour. Also, no reference seems to be made to this event at his trial; had it been seen a clear messianic claim, it would have been an easy piece of evidence against him. In addition, a public display of this kind would seem quite out of character with everything else Jesus had done thus far. Certainly in private, with his disciples, he made oblique statements about his purpose and destiny in Jerusalem, but he often pushed worship and adulation away from himself, saying, for example, that only God is good and only God may be worshipped.

What was the crowd's perception? If they'd been chanting that the Son of David was coming, it would certainly have been a messianic statement, but they weren't singing and shouting about the Son of David or 'the kingdom of God' that Jesus had always preached about. Instead they were talking of 'the coming kingdom of our ancestor David'. In the week of Passover, this makes sense as a statement of hope and longing for the fulfilment of God's promises, but it doesn't claim that Jesus is the Messiah. At least as far as the crowd and the city authorities were concerned, it seems that the entry into Jerusalem was less likely to have been organised around Jesus than to have been an existing pilgrimage walk that Jesus joined.

By the time the Gospel writers wrote it down, though, they were looking back on events with a richer interpretation. Both

Matthew and John connect Jesus' entry into Jerusalem with Zechariah's messianic prophecy: 'Rejoice greatly, O daughter Zion! Shout aloud, O daughter Jerusalem! Lo, your king comes to you; triumphant and victorious is he, humble and riding on a donkey, on a colt, the foal of a donkey' (Zechariah 9:9).

In the ancient world, a king making a triumphant entry into an arena would ride a white stallion. He would make no attempts at humility; he would not be deferring his glory to God or telling people not to mention his identity to anyone. That's not what kings did—but Jesus always turned people's expectations of him upside down. They expected a dour John the Baptist figure in a hair shirt, but what they got was a man who went to parties and turned water into wine. They expected a Messiah who would overthrow Rome, but what they got was a man who told them to put their weapons down. They expected a Messiah who would proclaim himself king, but what they got was a man who told them not to tell anyone who they thought he was. So, like everything else he touched, Jesus turned this moment upside down, too. He could not have been less like a king in the way he behaved. He was a servant king, not one who puts others in servitude; a king on a donkey, not on a stallion.

The crowds, then, were happy to see Jesus, but seem not to have been aware of anything more than that this popular and controversial preacher and miracle worker was making his pilgrimage into Jerusalem with everyone else. Although Jesus himself may have had some inner sense that he was entering the city as its Messiah, he certainly had no intention of being the kind of Messiah the crowd was hoping for. The disciples had been listening for some time to Jesus' oblique references to suffering and death and resurrection. Maybe they were beginning to add together the symbolism of kings on horses and the prophecy of the peaceable Messiah riding a donkey's colt. But even they, surely, still didn't foresee what would happen a few days later. They didn't expect to see a Messiah on a cross, any more than they expected to see a king on a donkey.

Angry Monday

Then they came to Jerusalem. And [Jesus] entered the temple and began to drive out those who were selling and those who were buying in the temple, and he overturned the tables of the money-changers and the seats of those who sold doves; and he would not allow anyone to carry anything through the temple. He was teaching and saying, 'Is it not written, "My house shall be called a house of prayer for all the nations"? But you have made it a den of robbers.' And when the chief priests and the scribes heard it, they kept looking for a way to kill him; for they were afraid of him, because the whole crowd was spellbound by his teaching. And when evening came, Jesus and his disciples went out of the city.

MARK 11:15–19

In the 1989 film *Jesus of Montreal*, a small group of actors is invited to reinvent the traditional Passion plays for Holy Week. The actors are not particularly devout but they engage fully with the Gospel stories in order to bring them to life. In doing so, they seem to capture something of the radical nature of the gospel. By contrast, the Church is portrayed as an utterly hypocritical institution, which has lost touch with the power of its own message. The actors decide to abandon the outdated tableau style of the traditional play and act out the Gospel stories realistically, and, as they enter into the spirit of the stories, they begin to have parallel experiences in everyday life, almost as if engaging with the Gospels with such honesty cannot fail to have a transforming effect on them.

In one scene, one of the female actors auditions for a TV advert and finds herself on the receiving end of some of the abuse that is common in that business. The actor who plays Jesus accompanies her to the audition and, when he sees her being exploited, steps in fearlessly to protect his friend. He trashes the studio, turning over the tables and tripods, smashing cameras and computers as he goes along, his anger growing with every step. This is not the calm and peaceful demonstration that a caricature of Jesus might suggest; it's clearly an act of criminal violence.

I recently showed this film to a group of theology students in Cambridge and, when it was finished, one of them voiced what many of us must have thought—that the traditional way to think of Christianity is that you aren't allowed to get angry, feel passionate or care so much about something that it leads to radical, unorthodox and criminal action.

I love the *Jesus of Montreal* adaptation of the biblical story because it delivers an image of the kind of passion and commitment to the cause of righteousness that makes Jesus (or his followers) fearless even against the powers that be. According to Matthew, Mark and Luke, the day Jesus turned over the tables in the temple was the day after Palm Sunday. Temple worship involved giving sacrifices—sometimes of money, which needed to be in the right currency, and sometimes of animals. Which kind of animal you were expected to sacrifice would depend on whether you were rich or poor. Consequently there were stalls lined up in the entrance to the temple, offering currency exchange and the sale of animals and birds, not offered purely as a service to the worshippers but as a means of making as much money as possible for the traders.

Jesus must have seen these stalls plenty of times on previous visits to the temple. Why he began destroying the tables on this particular visit isn't explained to us, but his action is one of outrage at the sight of injustice and commercialisation masquerading as religion, and he seems to have decided that peaceful demonstration wouldn't meet the occasion. He didn't just stand there and preach; he began to trash the stalls and scatter the merchandise.

The audition scene in the film captures the same kind of atmosphere as this scene in the temple, where, for the sake of a few people making a great deal of money, others are dehumanised and treated with injustice. The parallel with the story of the money-changers is beautifully drawn, for it demonstrates that the point Jesus made was about something bigger than just respect for a religious institution. Jesus was outraged that injustice was blatantly on show in the temple— the place that, more than anywhere else, symbolised the presence of God.

It's easy to fall into the habit of caricaturing the 'God of the Old Testament' as full of wrath and judgment, and the 'God of the New Testament', as seen in the life of Jesus, as kind and forgiving, liberating and pleasant. In fact, this tendency is only a short step from the fourth-century heresy of Marcion, who believed that the God of the Old Testament should be abandoned altogether and was even pretty choosy about which portions of the New Testament he believed we should retain. One of the good things about the story we've read here, however, is that it draws together love and forgiveness with a level of anger against injustice and corruption, without which love is so weak as to be almost meaningless. If by 'wrath' we mean uncontrollable, victimising, bullying anger, then we need to eliminate it. At the same time, though, we can see this story as a corrective to that view of Old Testament wrath versus New Testament love. Let's not forget, also, that the God of the Old Testament forgave and was tender towards his children.

While I wouldn't recommend that we should go out and commit random acts of criminal violence in the name of Jesus, I do think we should register Jesus' level of anger and understand how socially unacceptable his behaviour was on this occasion. We may sometimes be guilty in Holy Week of painting Jesus in pastel colours, as the lamb led to the slaughter. But the level of emotional and physical strength displayed here shows that, faced with continued injustice, he acted boldly, despite knowing that his actions were putting him in considerable danger. However difficult it is to define holiness, one thing is clear: it doesn't mean wet and wimpish, or meek and mild.

Crashed-out Tuesday

Six days before the Passover Jesus came to Bethany, the home of Lazarus, whom he had raised from the dead. There they gave a dinner for him. Martha served, and Lazarus was one of those at the table with him. Mary took a pound of costly perfume made of pure nard, anointed Jesus' feet, and wiped them with her hair. The house was filled with the fragrance of the perfume. But Judas Iscariot, one of his disciples (the one who was about to betray him), said, 'Why was this perfume not sold for three hundred denarii and the money given to the poor?' (He said this not because he cared about the poor, but because he was a thief; he kept the common purse and used to steal what was put into it.) Jesus said, 'Leave her alone. She bought it so that she might keep it for the day of my burial. You always have the poor with you, but you do not always have me.'

JOHN 12:1–8

Bethany is on the outskirts of Jerusalem, and, as the home of Jesus' great friends Lazarus, Martha and Mary, it was where he went as soon as he arrived in Jerusalem. Here, in this final week of his life, he took time away from the crowds to relax with his friends.

There's something so good about being with long-time friends, people with whom you've grown up and shared significant life experiences like going to university or raising your children. I recently began to feel the threads unravelling in my own daily life. I was extremely tired at the end of a long, busy term at university, with a publisher's deadline approaching and some intense meetings coming up in the weeks ahead. I was struggling to stay focused and just get everything done each day. I've learnt a long slow lesson in life, though—that when I'm this tired, what I need is not to work longer and harder to meet the deadline, but to stop for a break and recharge the batteries. So I called some friends who live near the sea, people I've known since I lived in London in my 20s. We have a lot of history in common; we know a lot of the same people and the same territory. We've seen each other's kids arrive and swapped notes through the struggles of parenting and career changes, and there's a lot of affection between us. As I strolled through their front door that Saturday afternoon, it felt as if a weight began to fall off my back. Why? Well, partly because I was 'away from it all' and there was nothing much I had to do for 24 hours. Mostly, though, it was because, unlike the kind of mental effort you have to put into meeting new people, with long-term, established friendships there's a level of relaxation that meets a fundamental human need.

This, I imagine, is why Jesus went to Bethany. At the end of a long journey, sensing that the day was coming when the pressure around his ministry would come to a head, he had a look around the temple in the evening and then went to his friends' place (Mark 11:11). There his friends did what they did best: Lazarus sat with him at the table, Martha served them, and Mary resumed her habit of sitting at his feet, listening to him talk.

I like the fact that the emphasis here is on what others did for him. It's easy to put the spotlight on what Jesus does for us, but this is another little glimpse into the way he lived out his life as a real human being. On this occasion, there was an extra and unusual element in what Jesus received from his friends. He was used to their hospitality, eating at their table and bringing a crowd of friends with him. This time, however, Mary didn't just listen but made an extraordinary gesture with a jar of perfume, something that was not only generous in the extreme but full of symbolism.

Virtually every street market in England has a stall selling imitation perfumes. They look and smell like the real thing but usually the smell doesn't develop in the same way and doesn't last so well. It was the same in the ancient world: nard was one of the most expensive perfumes available, and there were plenty of cheaper substitutes for it. Pliny the Elder wrote that nard-like perfumes were produced from no fewer than twelve different species of plant. Real nard, though, was made from the root of spikenard, a flowering plant that grows in the Himalayas, and was as expensive as it was rare. Nard was used in worship, being one of the eleven ingredients of the incense used in the temple at Jerusalem and also in temple worship in ancient Egypt. There was great excitement when a jar of perfume was found, still intact, in the tomb of King Tutankhamun. Analysis showed that it was pure nard, confirming previous theories that it was used at royal burials. In some forms of traditional medicine, nard is used to treat emotional pain and deep-seated grief; it's also used in palliative care to ease the transition from life to death. Mary, then, anointed Jesus with the precious oil that was associated with grief and pain, with the ointment that ushers in the time of death. With nard she was anointing a king for his burial and offering up worship to him as God.

More than anything else, though, nard was famous for its value—and Mary's jar of pure nard wasn't just a little jar; it was a whole pound of nard, more than half a kilo. Imagine the size of two packets of butter—that much of one of the most expensive perfumes available. Whatever it symbolised in terms of worship and kingship, for Mary it represented her life's savings, her dowry, her future, her pension, her prospects.

It's interesting that Jesus simply let her carry on pouring it out on his feet. He didn't stop her; he didn't say, 'It's OK, Mary, you don't need to do that. I know you love me but save some of this to look after your own interests.' He just received her extravagant, completely over-the-top act of adoration. This tells us something about Jesus' own needs. He knew events were coming to a crisis, he needed to be loved and cared for by his friends at this crucial point in his life, and he allowed them to pour themselves out for him. If even Jesus needed that, how much do we need it? It's something worth remembering when we're tempted to be self-sufficient under stress.

We should also bear in mind that Mary's act doesn't represent a daily habit of worship. This was a once-in-a-lifetime act of generosity, something she'd never done before and would never be able to repeat. Perhaps she, too, sensed the enormity of what was to come and knew, deep down, that this was her last chance to express her love for Jesus. If we have something precious to give to God, which represents all that we have, then we too need a sense of the right time to give it.

If we're to give our lives in the service of God, we do need to be willing to offer everything we have for him, but we need to choose our moment. We can only pour out our life's resources so many times. We need to know and understand the value of what we have—not just our possessions but our gifts and talents, our time, the welfare of our children and family, all that makes up our 'fortune'. We often hear gospel messages about being willing to give more, and about not hoarding what we have, and these are good messages. Equally, if we keep on pouring out all that we have without a thought for the timing or the effect, we may find ourselves at a moment of great significance with nothing left to give.

Outside looking in

Simon Peter was following Jesus, and so was another disciple. Now that disciple was known to the high priest, and entered with Jesus into the court of the high priest, but Peter was standing at the door outside. So the other disciple, who was known to the high priest, went out and spoke to the doorkeeper, and brought Peter in.

Then the slave-girl who kept the door said to Peter, 'You are not also one of this man's disciples, are you?' He said, 'I am not.' Now the slaves and the officers were standing there, having made a charcoal fire, for it was cold and they were warming themselves; and Peter was also with them, standing and warming himself... So they said to him, 'You are not also one of His disciples, are you?' He denied it, and said, 'I am not.' One of the slaves of the high priest, being a relative of the one whose ear Peter cut off, said, 'Did I not see you in the garden with Him?' Peter then denied it again, and immediately a rooster crowed.

JOHN 18:15–18, 25–27 (NASB)

Of all the disciples, Peter was one of the three closest to Jesus—a personal friend, not just a follower. He was also, as we have seen, a man of conviction. It was Peter who first declared his belief that Jesus was the Messiah (Mark 8:29); it was Peter who got out of the boat and walked on the water

(Matthew 14:28–29); and, when Jesus was arrested in the garden of Gethsemane, it was Peter who leapt to his defence and attacked one of the guards with a sword (John 18:10). Peter's impulsiveness was both his strength and his weakness. He lived out his beliefs with uncompromising passion but was inclined to trip over his own shoelaces. The story of his denial is a perfect illustration. Peter didn't betray Jesus in the same way that Judas did, with malice aforethought. Peter's denial was a spur-of-the-moment error, a misfire made within a grand attempt to be loyal and brave. Jesus saw it coming: he knew that Peter would jump too high and land with a crash (John 13:37–38). It seems that Jesus knew Peter better than he knew himself.

On the night Jesus was arrested, most of his disciples promptly disappeared into the shadows (Matthew 26:56). Only two of the disciples stuck around. That's the first thing to bear in mind about Peter: he ended up making an error only because he stayed close to Jesus in the first place. We can't be sure who the 'other disciple' was, although it's likely to have been John himself. When they took Jesus to the high priest's official residence, this other disciple had connections with the high priest, so it was easy for him to follow into the house with Jesus. Peter had also gone with them as far as the residence but found himself left outside while everyone else went through the gates.

Most of us, at some time in our lives, have felt that we are outside, looking in. We've stood on the sidelines at a social event where it seemed that everyone else was having a wonderful time, or attended church but never quite felt part of the in-crowd, or heard laughter coming from neighbours' windows and wondered whether other people have quite different and better lives than our own. At times like that, we're left wondering about the missing element: what is the code that we didn't learn, the privilege we didn't inherit, the quality we lack? Why are the others inside and we are on the outside?

When I was first an undergraduate at Cambridge, I was so overawed by the place that I couldn't quite believe it wasn't some accident that I was there at all. It seemed to me that everyone fitted in except me, and I must have been let in by mistake. Gradually, though, I began to find my feet with the work and make some friends, and I soon discovered that many others had the same experience. They had felt they were too dull and ordinary to be there; they too felt that they must have been admitted through some clerical error.

From Peter's perspective, it might have seemed that the other disciple's confidence, the way he strolled easily into high places, made his status as a follower of Jesus somehow more legitimate, more real, than his own. I can't help wondering whether Peter, left on the outside, began to dwell on his lack of privilege and finesse, his lack of connections and influence, his ordinary background as a simple fisherman from a northern, rural town.

It turned out that the first disciple was just as faithful a friend to Peter as he was to Jesus. Realising that Peter had been left behind, he went back to get him admitted, too. For some reason, though, even when Peter was allowed into the residence, he still didn't follow all the way to where Jesus was. Even within the walls of the house, he still remained something of an outsider. Maybe it was a feeling of insecurity that made this stubbornly loyal man suddenly deny all knowledge of Jesus. Peter, always the first to speak and act in support of Jesus, and fearless of making public statements about his faith, now speaks just as impulsively in denial, simply to save his own skin. In this moment of danger he attempts what is ultimately impossible—to stay faithful only in private.

As one of only two disciples who had followed Jesus this far, Peter ended by denying Jesus in public precisely because his passionate commitment had got him into danger. Having come so close to being a hero, his denial came as a revelation to himself of the cracks and flaws in his own make-up. Our relationships, with God and with other people, are similarly prone to failure when the present seems full of danger and the future is uncertain. In such moments of ambiguity, we too can find ourselves caught between the longing to be strong and committed and the fear that we'll be abandoned, bullied, ridiculed, injured or worse.

Weeks later, after the resurrection, Jesus met Peter on a beach and restored the relationship with three questions about love, one for each denial (John 21:15–17). It surely wasn't hard for Jesus to see the difference between Peter's denial, which came from a failure of nerve, and Judas' premeditated betrayal. He knew that beneath that complex mix of strength and weakness beat the heart of a man who longed to follow. Jesus had already forgiven so much of other people and, despite the fact that it's sometimes easier to forgive your enemies than your friends, he saw Peter's sorrow and love, and was tender-hearted towards him. The real challenge was for Peter to forgive himself.

Jesus' restoration of Peter—and of us, too—involves more than the simple forgiveness of failings and wrongdoings. It also requires a restoration of confidence. Forgiveness involves healing those things that make it impossible for us to live up to our own dreams and aspirations. Jesus makes us holy not merely by cancelling out our flaws but by giving us the ability to be more fully human, so that we can take our place in the world with greater confidence.

I love the fact that the Gospel stories are not full of plaster saints. They tell us about disciples who doubted and fled in fear, and they tell us about Peter, who stayed more faithful than most but still denied his friend and Lord at the last minute. As he realised he'd failed Jesus and let himself down so badly, he wept bitterly. We too will probably have moments of profound regret, but, as we dry our tears and accept that we're forgiven, we can thank God that he is not looking for plaster saints, but real ones.

Borrowed room; bread and wine

Then came the day of Unleavened Bread, on which the Passover lamb had to be sacrificed. So Jesus sent Peter and John, saying, 'Go and prepare the Passover meal for us that we may eat it.' They asked him, 'Where do you want us to make preparations for it?' 'Listen,' he said to them, 'when you have entered the city, a man carrying a jar of water will meet you; follow him into the house he enters and say to the owner of the house, "The teacher asks you, 'Where is the guest room, where I may eat the Passover with my disciples?'" He will show you a large room upstairs, already furnished. Make preparations for us there.' So they went and found everything as he had told them; and they prepared the Passover meal.

When the hour came, he took his place at the table, and the apostles with him. He said to them, 'I have eagerly desired to eat this Passover with you before I suffer; for I tell you, I will not eat it until it is fulfilled in the kingdom of God.' Then he took a cup, and after giving thanks he said, 'Take this and divide it among yourselves; for I tell you that from now on I will not drink of the fruit of the vine until the kingdom of God comes.' Then he took a loaf of bread, and when he had given thanks, he broke it and gave it to them, saying, 'This is my body, which is given for you. Do this in remembrance of me.' And he did the same with the cup after supper, saying, 'This cup that is poured out for you is the new covenant in my blood. But see, the one who betrays me is with me, and his hand is on the table. For the Son of Man is going as it has been determined, but woe to that one by whom he is betrayed!' Then they began to ask one another which one of them it could be who would do this.

LUKE 22:7–23

There have been a number of hints this week that Jesus constantly overturned popular ideas about kings and messiahs. He entered the city not in majesty on a white stallion but quietly on a donkey, blending in with a pilgrimage. When Mary anointed him with perfume fit for a king's burial, her sister and brother didn't turn a hair as she poured out the family wealth, but one of Jesus' own followers promptly commented that it was a shocking waste of money. We've sneaked a preview at Peter's restoration and found that, while any other king would surely shout 'treason' if one of his closest courtiers denied him, Jesus looked deep into the heart of his friend and forgave him.

The borrowed room and the bread and wine also act to disrupt our expectations. Luke frames Jesus' life, using the motif of the borrowed room like a pair of brackets. He told of Jesus entering the city of David just in time for his birth, where his parents sought shelter in an inn, or guest room, and were told there was no room for them there. The city of David there referred to Bethlehem, King David's ancestral home. Now, as the end of his life approaches, Jesus enters the other city of David—Jerusalem, King David's capital city. Jesus sends his disciples to look for a room to celebrate the Passover, which he knows will mark the end of his life. The 'upper room' is from the same word in Greek that is rendered 'inn' or 'guest room' in Luke 2:7—*kataluma*. Jesus began and ended his life in borrowed rooms—not a king in a palace or a priest in a temple, but a man with his friends in a borrowed space.

The supper they shared in the borrowed room was not just any old supper but the Passover—a meal by which the Jews commemorated their national and religious tradition. They retold the story of God leading them out of Egypt from slavery to promise, not just as a piece of social history but as the story of salvation. The food and the order in which it was eaten were symbolic, in terms of both the exodus story and their hope for the future. Lamb was eaten with bitter herbs, commemorating the bitterness of slavery, following the commandment of Exodus 12:8. Bread was made without yeast, to remember that the journey from Egypt was made in such a hurry that the people didn't have time to let their bread rise. Later, another tradition grew up that yeast was symbolic of sin, and so all traces of yeast would be cleared from the house before Passover began.

The bread that Jesus broke and shared was not just a piece of unleavened bread from the table, however. It was a particular piece of bread—'the' bread, which was set aside, with a special cup, never touched or drunk by anyone at the table. *The* bread and *the* cup symbolised the fulfilment of the promise that Elijah would return, the hope of the coming Messiah. When Jesus took that bread and that cup, he wasn't just instituting a form of fellowship or suggesting that whenever we eat together we should remember him. He was taking these traditional symbols of the future hope of salvation and investing them with new significance.

Christians have argued for centuries about how Holy Communion should be celebrated. Should we believe that the bread and wine are mystically transformed, or should we stay rational and practical and insist that they are merely a commemoration of what Jesus did for us on the cross? Should we use wine or something non-alcoholic; wafers, to save sacred crumbs from falling to the floor, or real bread to symbolise the reality of the feast? How much liberty should we take in reinterpreting the feast: do rice and saki, or cake and lemonade weaken the symbolism or make it more meaningful in different cultures?

To unwrap those questions in detail is the task of a different book, but I like the comment Karl Barth made about Communion. A Protestant theologian, he was challenged as to whether he believed in the presence of Christ at the Eucharist. In reply, Barth said that he had, in some sense, to believe in Christ's presence in the Eucharist. Why? Because to deny it was to suggest that Christ was absent from the Eucharist, and that he could not believe.

Celebrating worship with physical elements, the bread and the wine, matters because it affirms that our worship is not merely cerebral, not just conceptual, not a matter of words spoken and ideas agreed upon. Our worship cannot be separated from our physical existence. Our meeting with Christ is not just in words but in flesh and blood, an incarnate reality just as Jesus himself was the Word made flesh. Eating and drinking the bread and wine gives us a way of enacting physically the fact that God is a reality in our lives; it stops us reducing our worship merely to a reiteration of beliefs; it offers a way of worshipping with the heart and body and soul, and not just the mind (Mark 12:30).

Borrowed rooms, bread and wine: these elements marked the last supper as a feast of the disruption of ideas, and they continue to overturn the tendency towards smoothing things into a predictable religious format. Holy Communion is neither magic nor superstition; nor is it a ritual whose meaning is lost in history. Rather, it's about connecting us to a flesh-and-blood reality.

Bad Friday

When it was noon, darkness came over the whole land until three in the afternoon. At three o'clock Jesus cried out with a loud voice, 'Eloi, Eloi, lema sabachthani?' which means, 'My God, my God, why have you forsaken me?' When some of the bystanders heard it, they said, 'Listen, he is calling for Elijah.' And someone ran, filled a sponge with sour wine, put it on a stick, and gave it to him to drink, saying, 'Wait, let us see whether Elijah will come to take him down.' Then Jesus gave a loud cry and breathed his last. And the curtain of the temple was torn in two, from top to bottom. Now when the centurion, who stood facing him, saw that in this way he breathed his last, he said, 'Truly this man was God's Son!'

There were also women looking on from a distance; among them were Mary Magdalene, and Mary the mother of James the younger and of Joses, and Salome. These used to follow him and provided for him when he was in Galilee; and there were many other women who had come up with him to Jerusalem.

MARK 15:33–41

'Why is it called *Good* Friday?' asked my son when he was seven years old. 'It's not good at all, it's really, *really* bad.' Reading the story in his children's Bible, he was quite upset at the plight of 'poor Jesus'.

For adults, too, there is the temptation to move swiftly over the agonising picture of the death of Jesus and reassure ourselves with a happy ending, but the impact of Good Friday is snatched away if we rush too quickly to the promise of resurrection. We should dwell on the dreadful spectre of Good Friday and all the ripples that go out from it—not just its meaning in terms of our spiritual salvation but its connection to the injustices of the world, the suffering of innocents, the evil of regimes that keep tight control over people's lives and end up murdering them, body and soul. It's equally true that we can lessen the outrageous, unimaginable joy of Sunday if we dampen it down by returning too soon to the cross. There's a time for everything—a time to laugh and a time to weep, a time for joy and a time for sadness—and we miss something if we don't allow ourselves to be met by each chapter in turn as the story unfolds.

Today we remember Jesus' suffering and death by crucifixion. He stood for life and love and justice and faith, upsetting convention and exposing hypocrisy, until the world couldn't stand it and tried to stamp it out of him. The Early Fathers saw this death as God's trick against the devil: the devil wanted him dead but failed to understand that the Son of God cannot remain dead for long—something not unlike the 'deep magic' and the 'magic deeper still' of which C.S. Lewis wrote in *The Lion, the Witch and the Wardrobe*.[9]

It's important to realise, though, that the disciples of Jesus (and, to a certain extent, Jesus himself) could not see beyond the moment. Gradually, after the event, it was overlaid with layers of theological meaning, which were crystallised when the Gospels were written down. John's account emphasises Jesus' victory over death so strongly that Jesus seems to be in control, and perhaps slightly above the impact of the suffering. Matthew makes connections with messianic prophecies and theological meaning, while Luke pays close attention to the impact of the crucifixion on other people. Of the four Gospel writers, Mark is the one who best conveys a sense of the sheer human suffering and agony of the cross.

There are similar differences of interpretation in depictions of the cross in art. In the early centuries of Christianity, the cross wasn't used as a symbol of Christianity, precisely because it was an instrument of torture as well as a means of execution. Crucifixion was such an agonising and humiliating death that it was not used for citizens of the Roman Empire, except for traitors, and eventually it was banned because it was so barbaric. Later, depictions of the cross became central to religious art, but representations were largely symbolic. Take a trip round any Western art gallery and you're bound to find medieval paintings of a clean, white Jesus hanging from a cross with a scratch or two on his otherwise strong-looking body. The portrayal of the ugly reality of crucifixion entered the world of religious art only quite recently.

One of the most heart-rending images of the cross is *The Tortured Christ* by Brazilian sculptor Guido Rocha. The beaten and battered body of Jesus hangs from the cross with every sinew stretched against pain and his face contorted in screams of agony and rage, which not only vividly portrays Jesus' own suffering but also deliberately links the cross with the sufferings of religious or political prisoners who are being tortured to death at this very moment.

Like Mark's stark telling of the story, Rocha's sculpture produces a sense of horror and revulsion by focusing on Jesus' human experience there and then, rather than reflecting on its theological meaning after the event. Images such as this remind us with a shock that true Christianity is not comfortable, conventional or respectable. It's a faith that demands radical action, will at least cost us some kind of sacrifice and may cause us degrees of pain. Is that the kind of faith we are prepared to take on?

Both Mark and Rocha call to mind the fact that Jesus endured real, vile torture to the point of death. So, as we remember Jesus' agony, let's also pray with compassion and act with courage on behalf of those who are victims of torture somewhere in the world today. How? Each one of us has to find that out. But when we look at religious imagery like this, something is lacking if we say in our prayers that we long to take Jesus down from the cross and end his suffering, but we don't do the same for those suffering today. That's not just a 'social gospel'; it's the call of Jesus himself, when he said:

'I was hungry, and you gave Me something to eat; I was thirsty, and you gave Me something to drink; I was a stranger, and you invited Me in; naked, and you clothed Me; I was sick, and you visited Me; I was in prison, and you came to Me… Truly I say to you, to the extent that you did it to one of these brothers of Mine, even to the least of them, you did it to Me.' (Matthew 25:35–36, 40, NASB)

The absence of God

After these things, Joseph of Arimathea, who was a disciple of Jesus, though a secret one because of his fear of the Jews, asked Pilate to let him take away the body of Jesus. Pilate gave him permission; so he came and removed his body. Nicodemus, who had at first come to Jesus by night, also came, bringing a mixture of myrrh and aloes, weighing about a hundred pounds. They took the body of Jesus and wrapped it with the spices in linen cloths, according to the burial custom of the Jews. Now there was a garden in the place where he was crucified, and in the garden there was a new tomb in which no one had ever been laid. And so, because it was the Jewish day of Preparation, and the tomb was nearby, they laid Jesus there.

JOHN 19:38–42

For weeks now, the shops have been full of chocolate eggs and chickens and sunshine and cheer. Yet Good Friday and Holy Saturday are the most sombre days in the whole Church calendar, recalling the death of Jesus and the absence of God. We've touched a few times in this Lenten journey on the idea of God seeming to disappear—Moses seeing God only through clouds, Job wondering where God is when it hurts, and the disciples rowing across the sea and wondering why Jesus has left them to perish.

Here we read of two of Jesus' disciples dealing with the death. It's not clear why these two lesser-known disciples went to claim the body, rather than Peter, James and John, but it's interesting to notice that, as dusk began to fall on the eve of Holy Saturday, the two disciples who dealt with the body were the two secret followers of Jesus. Nicodemus had already had a conversation with Jesus in the darkness. Now, together with Joseph, he comes in the first shadows of evening to carry out this reverent act of love on the day when the light of the world was extinguished.

A burial would usually have taken some time, and they would have hurried to finish before nightfall and the beginning of the sabbath. They dressed the body and laid it in the nearest tomb, as there was no time to go further afield. Then there was silence. Nothing at all. There could be no activity on the next day, Holy Saturday, because it was the sabbath. A whole day of darkness and silence elapsed and there is nothing of the story to tell.

For those who enjoy a degree of certainty in their faith, it may be that the blankness of Holy Saturday doesn't really 'bite': it may simply be a day of anticipation of the joy that is to come. But that first Saturday was a day of utter devastation. Not only had the disciples witnessed the shocking, violent death of their friend and beloved leader; there was also the fact that, while following Jesus, they had dreamed of a different future—a future when they would no longer live under Roman occupation, a future when their religious structures would loosen up and encompass the poor and the sick and the marginalised, a future when the hungry would be fed and the land of promise would again be a land that would ring with the praises of God. They had lost not only their friend and leader but their dreams as well.

It may seem maudlin to reflect too deeply on such things

but, without wishing to dwell gratuitously on the violence, it is surely healthy to keep a day and a half a year when we acknowledge the awful impact of Jesus' death. To turn immediately to the resurrection is like a denial of reality, but to contemplate the sense of God's absence that the disciples must have felt may have a spiritual value for us.

For those of us who live with a fragmented faith, a faith that has had too many holes punctured in it by circumstances, too much damage ever to return to a simplistic certainty, there is something healing about living through the rise and fall of the Church seasons. It's a relief to acknowledge the disappearance of God on Holy Saturday and the uncertainty of the outcome. That's not to say that we remove ourselves from the hope of the resurrection, but we admit that hope doesn't prevent the bleakness of God's apparent absence from descending even upon those with the strongest faith. C.S. Lewis wrote in *A Grief Observed* that when you are happy and feel no particular need of God, he seems to be there and welcoming you with open arms:

But go to Him when your need is desperate, when all other help is vain, and what do you find? A door slammed in your face, and a sound of bolting and double bolting on the inside. After that, silence. You may as well turn away. The longer you wait, the more emphatic the silence will become. [10]

As their hopes for a new future evaporated overnight, the disciples faced instead a great chasm of grief as God vanished from sight with no promise that he would ever return. The magnitude of grief they faced on Holy Saturday was because they believed that Jesus was gone forever.

It's a common experience, when people are first bereaved, that they do not feel the impact of the loss. Their loved one still feels present to them; the death hasn't yet had time to sink in. There is a great deal to be done just to organise a funeral, and in those first few days they can be swept along, carried by the warmth and sympathy and kind words of friends. It's often a few days after the funeral that the real bleakness begins. Friends and relatives return to their normal routine, and the bereaved person has to go back to theirs— except that, for them, nothing will ever be normal again. That's when the absence of the loved one starts to become real, as a strange and unwelcome future opens up like a blank white page.

This is what Holy Saturday is: the absence of God, and the uncertainty and emptiness of being uprooted. Easter faith was born in the darkness and, like the disciples, sometimes we just have to wait in the shadows until eventually a glimmer of light appears on the horizon.

Questions for reflection

- What are the injustices in our society that need a bold or even shocking response?
- What gifts and treasures do I have, that should only be given away thoughtfully?
- What can we do to help bring release to those who suffer injustice and pain?
- What are the shadows we live under, that make it impossible to see God?

Gone fishing

After these things Jesus showed himself again to the disciples by the Sea of Tiberias; and he showed himself in this way. Gathered there together were Simon Peter, Thomas called the Twin, Nathanael of Cana in Galilee, the sons of Zebedee, and two others of his disciples. Simon Peter said to them, 'I am going fishing.' They said to him, 'We will go with you.' They went out and got into the boat, but that night they caught nothing.

Just after daybreak, Jesus stood on the beach; but the disciples did not know that it was Jesus. Jesus said to them, 'Children, you have no fish, have you?' They answered him, 'No.' He said to them, 'Cast the net to the right side of the boat, and you will find some.' So they cast it, and now they were not able to haul it in because there were so many fish. That disciple whom Jesus loved said to Peter, 'It is the Lord!' When Simon Peter heard that it was the Lord, he put on some clothes, for he was naked, and jumped into the lake. But the other disciples came in the boat, dragging the net full of fish, for they were not far from the land, only about a hundred yards off.

When they had gone ashore, they saw a charcoal fire there, with fish on it, and bread. Jesus said to them, 'Bring some of the fish that you have just caught.' So Simon Peter went aboard and hauled the net ashore, full of large fish, a hundred and fifty-three of them; and though there were so many, the net was not torn. Jesus said to them, 'Come and have breakfast.' Now none of the disciples dared to ask him, 'Who are you?' because they knew it was the Lord. Jesus came and took the bread and gave it to them, and did the same with the fish. This was now the third time that Jesus appeared to the disciples after he was raised from the dead.

JOHN 21:1–14

The story of Easter morning took place in a garden, not on a beach, but I've chosen this story for Easter Day because, after the 46 days of Lent, we need to remember that Easter lasts even longer—not just one day but 50. The resurrection is only the beginning of new life; the weeks of resurrection appearances, the ascension, the waiting in Jerusalem for the coming of the Spirit—all these are part of Easter as well.

That first Easter, Jesus appeared to his disciples many times over the course of several weeks. Because the resurrection stories are told to us by different Gospel writers, it's impossible to piece together a proper chronology. This story sees seven of the disciples, all of them fishermen, back in Galilee where their fishing business was located.

Going back to work after a long time away can sometimes be a struggle and sometimes a relief, but I think Peter must have gone back to his fishing with quite mixed feelings. For a start, even though Jesus' death had been followed by the joy of his resurrection, there wasn't yet much clarity about what the disciples were going to do next, now that he wasn't with them any more. Were they supposed to carry on with the itinerant ministry, or go back to where they'd come from? They were probably living with a strange mixture of joy, regret and uncertainty until Peter, ever the practical one, broke the spell and announced that he was going back to work. So off they went to the beach.

Peter was done with grieving, done with trying to work out what to do next. The big dream was over—the hope of a Messiah to liberate them politically, the anticipation of a new kingdom, a new regime, a new order, a new life. Jesus was risen and that meant joy, but it didn't change the fact that life couldn't continue as it had done for the last couple of years. Somehow, they had to go back to their old lives and pick up where they'd left off.

Yet this fishing trip wasn't like before—this was different. Peter couldn't catch any fish. What was going on? Obviously there were always good nights and bad, but no fish *at all*? That seemed a bit rough on the first day back. Then, with a touch of déjà vu, there's a voice across the water: 'Try fishing on the other side of the boat.' Where had he heard that before? Of course there were always some jokers on the shore, shouting that there were fish over here, fish over there. Very funny. But that time Jesus had said it, there really had been a great haul of fish, so many that the nets couldn't hold them all.

'Those were the days,' thinks Peter to himself. 'I miss having him here, miss the way he always knew what to do, the way he would always surprise you, catch you out with something, make everything so much more alive than it was before.'

'Still,' he thinks, 'we may as well try the other side once more before we give up for the night.' So he throws the nets overboard one more time—feeling the pangs of memory, wondering if he'll ever stop missing his friend—and suddenly it's happening all over again. Not only are there fish on the other side of the boat but there's a ridiculous number of fish, hundreds of them, like a gift from God.

I imagine Peter turning round and squinting through the light of dawn to see the figure on the shore. It couldn't be, could it? Then there's a voice at his side: 'It's the Lord.' The disciple Jesus loved—he was always the first to know, like an intuition. Peter leaps out of the boat, not walking on the water this time but swimming to the shallows, then wading back to the shore. And it is him. There he is, with a fire and some fish ready, waiting for Peter to bring in some more.

Even going fishing, you see, was never going to be the same again. It wouldn't matter what Peter did from then on: none of it would ever be a matter of going back to what he'd done before. Everything would look different, smell different, taste different, because the Lord had been here. Jesus had walked through Peter's life, just as God had walked past Moses on the mountain top, and Peter had seen the glory of the Lord just as surely as Moses had. Peter could go fishing any time he liked—he would always be a fisherman. What he couldn't do was go backwards.

Recognising that Easter is 50 days long is important if, somehow, you've arrived at Easter morning and you don't feel overjoyed, don't feel much hope for the future. There are seasons in our lives when Lent is a more comfortable place to live, because it reflects our struggles and our doubts. There may be circumstances in your life that make you feel entirely out of step with the joy of Easter Sunday, but even if joy hasn't materialised for you yet, it's still a promise of things to come that will unfold in time. Easter is a promise that the absence of God has been penetrated with light, and the silence of the early morning is no longer hollow but hopeful, as if heaven is holding its breath, waiting for us. Even though we may still live with the frustration that all we can see (like Moses) is God's vanishing back, we know that we will, one day, look into his face.

We can never just go back to where we were before—back to the world, back to the church, back to life as if nothing has happened. Every place we've ever been will now look different because we've met Jesus.

Come and have breakfast. Lent is over, and Easter has only just begun.

Notes

1   Roald Dahl, *The BFG* (Jonathan Cape, 1982), p. 15.
2   Wilfred Owen, *The Complete Poems and Fragments*, ed. Jon Stallworthy (W.W. Norton, 1984).
3   John Cassian, *Conferences* (Paulist Press, 1998), pp. 81–100.
4   Antoine de Sainte Exupéry, *Le Petit Prince* (Mariner Books, French language edition, 2001), p. 65.
5   C.S. Lewis, *The Lion, The Witch and the Wardrobe* (Collins, 1950), p. 166.
6   Gregory of Nyssa, *Life of Moses* (Paulist Press, 1978), p. 93.
7   From 'Magnificat' in Noel Rowe, *Next to Nothing* (Vagabond Press, 2004).
8   Carl Honoré, *In Praise of Slow* (Orion, 2004), pp. 2–3
9   Lewis, *The Lion, the Witch and the Wardrobe,* p. 148
10 C.S. Lewis, *A Grief Observed* (Faber & Faber, 1961), p. 9

ENJOYED READING THIS LENT BOOK?

Did you know BRF publishes a new Lent and Advent book each year? All our Lent and Advent books are designed with a daily printed Bible reading, comment and reflection. Some can be used in groups and contain questions which can be used in a study or reading group.

Previous Lent books have included:

Fasting and Feasting, Gordon Giles
Journey to Jerusalem, David Winter
The Road to Emmaus, Helen Julian CSF
The Rainbow of Renewal, Michael Mitton

If you would like to be kept in touch with information about our forthcoming Lent or Advent books, please complete the coupon below.

❏ Please keep me in touch by post with forthcoming Lent or Advent books
❏ Please email me with details about forthcoming Lent or Advent books

Email address: _____

Name _____

Address_____

_____

_____

Postcode_____

Telephone_____

Signature _____

Please send this completed form to:

Freepost RRLH-JCYA-SZX
BRF, 15 The Chambers,
Vineyard, Abingdon,
OX14 3FE, United Kingdom

Tel. 01865 319700
Fax. 01865 319701
Email: enquiries@brf.org.uk

www.brf.org.uk

PROMO REF: END/LENT09

BRF is a Registered Charity

For more information, visit the **brf** website at **www.brf.org.uk**

Beginnings and Endings (and what happens in between)

Daily Bible readings from Advent to Epiphany

Advent is all about beginnings. It's the beginning of the Church year, and its themes include the beginning of creation, the beginning of Christianity, and the beginning of the new heaven and the new earth. Most of these beginnings are born out of the ending of something else—an old era giving way to a new one.

Our everyday lives are full of small-scale beginnings and endings—births, deaths, marriages, careers, house moves and so on. How do the grand-scale beginnings and endings of Advent help to guide us as we seek to follow Jesus in the 21st century? This book reflects on the stories of six groups of people and individual characters from the Bible; each provides a focus for the idea of beginnings and endings, and each gives us a glimpse into—and draws ancient wisdom from—the human experience that happened in between.

ISBN 978 1 84101 566 8   £7.99
Available from your local Christian bookshop or, in case of difficulty, direct from BRF using the order form on page 223.

Fasting and Feasting

Daily Bible readings
from Ash Wednesday to Easter Day

Gordon Giles

This book of daily Bible readings for Lent takes food as its focus, an ideal topic for the traditional time in the Church's year when our thoughts may turn to the spiritual discipline of fasting or at least abstaining from food and drink in some way. In the affluent West it is easy to take food for granted and forget that God may call us to account in this as well as other areas of our lives.

The Lenten fast concludes with the Easter feast, and along the way this book examines not only both fasting and feasting but a range of wider issues from hospitality to our stewardship of the world's resources. We also spend time reflecting on the two great symbolic meals of Old and New Testaments— the Passover and the Last Supper, where Jesus instituted the celebration of Holy Communion.

ISBN 978 1 84101 569 9   £7.99
Available from your local Christian bookshop or, in case of difficulty, direct from BRF using the order form on page 223.

Journey to Jerusalem

Bible readings
from Ash Wednesday to Easter Sunday

David Winter

'Twelve young men were walking with their leader along a road about 30 miles north of Galilee. As they walked, their leader put two questions to them, and the answer to the second one would have profound consequences not just for them but eventually for the whole world. The leader was Jesus. The twelve young men (and they were young, most of them barely in their 20s) were his disiples.'

This book follows the journey of Jesus and his followers to Jerusalem—the story of the culmination of his ministry in the events of Good Friday and Easter, the story of the 'good news of God' for the whole world. It is this story that shapes the faith and life of every Christian. As we reflect on these events, like the disciples we can experience the awakening of faith in Jesus and hear the challenge to follow him, wherever he leads.

ISBN 978 1 84101 485 2   £7.99
Available from your local Christian bookshop or, in case of difficulty, direct from BRF using the order form on page 223.

Seasons of the Spirit

One community's journey
through the Christian year

Teresa Morgan

'Watch and pray. Advent's motto is good for Lent, too. But I am too tired to pray: even the short step into silence seems a marathon. I am tempted to sit down under the chestnut tree, and hope that the new life which touches it one sunny morning will quicken me too. Instead, I turn homewards.'

This book is a journey through the seasons of the year and also through the high days and holy days of the Church. In the company of saints present and past, we travel from Advent Sunday to Advent Sunday, looking for the kingdom of heaven and reflecting on the many ways in which God's love reaches out to embrace and transform the world. Interspersing prose with poetry, this is a book to read slowly and reflectively, stilling our minds to the rhythms of grace and opening our hearts to the peace that passes all understanding.

ISBN 978 1 84101 710 5   £5.99
Available February 2010 from your local Christian bookshop or, in case of difficulty, direct from BRF using the order form on page 223.

Embracing a Concrete Desert

A spiritual journey towards wholeness

Lynne E. Chandler

'I wish I could say that I have arrived and will never have to stare into the darkness again, but I know that isn't so. I do know, though, that I have to embrace the present moment and celebrate life, whatever that may involve today. My Creator is alive within and throughout this amazing world, and has never failed to wrap me in wings of protection and comfort.'

This is the story of an unfinished journey—a journey that finds a path through struggle and difficulty to acceptance and peace of mind. It is the story of one woman choosing to seek wholeness despite heartache, serenity in the midst of struggling to adapt to a very different life, and discovering how in the driest of desert places God can reveal fresh water springs for the soul. It is a story shared through lyrical reflections and poems sparked by the ups and downs of life in a teeming Middle Eastern metropolis.

ISBN 978 1 84101 686 3   £5.99
Available January 2010 from your local Christian bookshop or, in case of difficulty, direct from BRF using the order form on page 223.

ORDERFORM

REF	TITLE	PRICE	QTY	TOTAL
566 8	Beginnings and Endings	£7.99		
569 9	Fasting and Feasting	£7.99		
485 2	Journey to Jerusalem	£7.99		
710 5	Seasons of the Spirit	£5.99		
686 3	Embracing a Concrete Desert	£5.99		

POSTAGE AND PACKING CHARGES				
Order value	UK	Europe	Surface	Air Mail
£7.00 & under	£1.25	£3.00	£3.50	£5.50
£7.10–£30.00	£2.25	£5.50	£6.50	£10.00
Over £30.00	FREE	prices on request		

Postage and packing	
Donation	
TOTAL	

Name _____ Account Number _____

Address _____

_____ Postcode _____

Telephone Number_____

Email _____

Payment by: ❏ Cheque ❏ Mastercard ❏ Visa ❏ Postal Order ❏ Maestro

Card no ❏❏❏❏ ❏❏❏❏ ❏❏❏❏ ❏❏❏❏ ❏❏❏

Valid from ❏❏❏❏ Expires ❏❏❏❏ Issue no. ❏❏❏

Security code* ❏❏❏ *Last 3 digits on the reverse of the card.
ESSENTIAL IN ORDER TO PROCESS YOUR ORDER   Shaded boxes for Maestro use only

Signature _____ Date _____

All orders must be accompanied by the appropriate payment.

Please send your completed order form to:
BRF, 15 The Chambers, Vineyard, Abingdon OX14 3FE
Tel. 01865 319700 / Fax. 01865 319701 Email: enquiries@brf.org.uk

❏ Please send me further information about BRF publications.

Available from your local Christian bookshop.   BRF is a Registered Charity

brf

Resourcing your spiritual journey

through...

- Bible reading notes
- Books for Advent & Lent
- Books for Bible study and prayer
- Books to resource those working with
  under 11s in school, church and at home

- Quiet days and retreats
- Training for primary teachers
  and children's leaders
- Godly Play
- Barnabas RE Days

For more information, visit the **brf** website at **www.brf.org.uk**